216921

12.99

NJ 4/02

BASIC DESIG
THE DYNAMI(
VISUAL FO

D0766199

Secrets of colour theory? Why call those principles, secrets, which all artists must know and all should have been taught?
Delacroix

Art is the demonstration that the ordinary is extraordinary.
Ozenfant

In art, progress lies not in an extension but in a knowledge of limitations
Braque

If you know before you see, you can't see for knowing.
Terry Frost

BASIC DESIGN:
THE DYNAMICS OF
VISUAL FORM

Maurice de Sausmarez

SECOND REVISED EDITION

Foreword by Gyorgy Kepes

A & C Black • London

Copyright © Maurice de Sausmarez 1964
© Jane de Sausmarez 1983, 2002
First edition reprinted 1964, 1965 (twice), 1966, 1967,
1968, 1970, 1973, 1974, 1975, 1976, 1978, 1980

First revised edition published in 1983 in Great Britain by
The Herbert Press Limited
Reprinted 1987, 1990, 1992

This second revised edition published in 2002 in Great Britain by
the Herbert Press, an imprint of A & C Black (Publishers) Ltd,
37 Soho Square, London W1D 3QZ

Designed by Jo Tapper
Cover design by Dorothy Moir
Printed and bound in Spain by
Graficas Reunidas, S.A.

All rights reserved. No part of this publication may be
reproduced or used in any form or by any means – graphic,
electronic or mechanical, including photocopying, recording,
taping or information storage and retrieval systems – without
permission of the publishers.

British Library Cataloguing in Publication Data
de Sausmarez, Maurice
Basic design.—Rev. ed.—(Design handbooks)
1. Aesthetics
I. Title II. Series
701.1'7 N66

ISBN 0 7136 5241 1

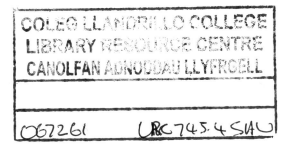

COLEG LLANDRILLO COLLEGE
LIBRARY RESOURCE CENTRE
CANOLFAN ADNODDAU LLYFRGELL

067261   LRC 745.4 SAU

CONTENTS

FOREWORD

It is not an easy task to write a fresh and convincing introductory text to the teaching of the visual arts today. Maurice de Sausmarez has done it. With admirable clarity and consistency, Basic design: the dynamics of visual form guides the reader through a range of problems that can potentially illuminate the issues which are significant in the unfolding of his visual creativity. Step by step, he takes the basic visual elements and relates them in an increasingly complex manner.

What differentiates his text from the plethora of visual art textbooks available today are: firstly, its clear and well-thought-out language; secondly, its well-coordinated sequence of ideas, through which each new situation opens up a wide new horizon; and, lastly, a rich complementarity of text and illustrations. The functions of word and image do not move parallel to one another, but act like a well-constructed dovetail joint, which gains strength by the very nature of its opposing forms acting as mutual reinforcements. What the text cannot do, the illustrations can; and the text confirms, extends and reinforces the meaning of the illustrations. In admirable sequence, through word and image, the author leads on from the exploration of graphic tools to an ever-increasing complexity of graphic forces.

Nicholas Poussin remarked in one of his letters that he took great pride that in his work he never neglected anything. Poussin's Cartesian clarity is echoed in Mr de Sausmarez's survey of the interconnected factors in spatial presentation. He examines all the possible complementary arrangements of visual elements, neglecting nothing. From problems of visual balance to visual kinetics, he exposes the reader to the various avenues of imaginative exploration – which is the major challenge a visual artist must face in his work.

We know that motor performance at the physical level, and work, which are the foundations of our social existence, are based upon the alternation of action and repose in a measure corresponding to the natural periods of breathing and neuro-muscular effort. Optimum performance is arrived at by a rhythmic articulation common to the body, the mind and the task. Emotional drive, muscular energy and technical knowledge become parts of a symmetrical relationship between man and man, and between man and nature, when a rhythm of action and repose synchronises ends and means, and also synchronises flesh, heart and brain. This synchronisation introduces a new quality of experience; work becoming something

plate 1
A painting based on studies of an industrial refuse disposal plant

far more than the mere fulfilment of an assigned task. The sensing of this unity is the germination of an experience basic to every form of art.

Maurice de Sausmarez's Basic Design is itself an art in this sense. More than the sum total of its parts, it is also much more than the mechanical interconnections of its elements. Its imaginative nature – that is, its ability to demonstrate the play of the various elements which constitute the structure of the work of art – is in itself a continuation of vision.

I believe that this book can act as essential yeast to raise and make fuller from within the reader's creative vision; and it is my sincere hope that it will have an ever-increasing readership.

Gyorgy Kepes, Professor of Visual Design
Massachusetts Institute of Technology

December 1982

AUTHOR'S ACKNOWLEDGEMENTS

I gratefully acknowledge all that I have gained from long friendship with Harry Thubron whose work in Leeds and with Art Foundation, London, has contributed much to art education. I am indebted to Professor Gyorgy Kepes, Associate Professor Preusser and the Massachusetts Institute of Technology for permission to include plates 6, 27, 64, 67, 91 from the courses in Visual Design; to William Culbert for the use of plates 88a and b.

I also wish to express my gratitude to the following artists who have generously allowed me to include work done by students under their direction: Denis Broodbank (Polytechnic School of Architecture, London) plates 24, 44, 61, 90; Robert Brazil (Goldsmith's College School of Art) plates 21, 31, 51, 83, 89; Oliffe Richmond (Chelsea School of Art) plates 25, 32, 43, 54a, 54b, 55, 56; Bridget Riley, plates 41, 77a and b; Peter Green, plates 68, 70a and b; John Flavin, plates 4, 52a, 58, 59, 62, 111; Wynn Jones, plates 1, 74, 75a and b; Jane Boswell; and to many of my own students whose work is illustrated.

PUBLISHERS' ACKNOWLEDGEMENTS

For this second edition, the Publishers are grateful to the Foundation Course, Faculty of Art and Design, Middlesex University (Course Head, Max Shepherd) for the permission to include plates 7, 8a and b, 11, 22, 23, 45, 52b and c, 57, 65a and b, 66, 80, and to the Camberwell School of Arts and Crafts for permission to illustrate work done by a sculpture student (plate 78b).

For this second revised edition the Publishers are also grateful to the Foundation Course, University College Northampton, (course leader Clive Ramsdale) for permission to include plates 2, 3, 9a and b, 10, 71a and b, 73, 79, 84 and 92.

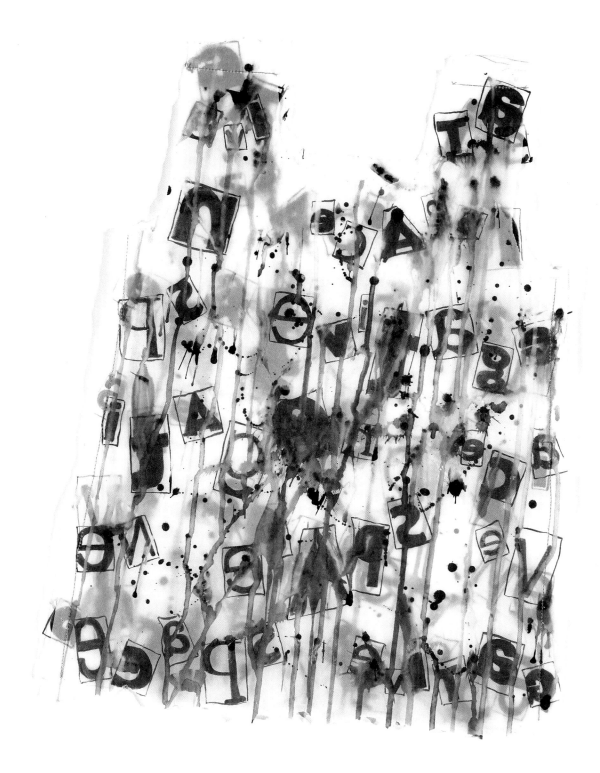

PREFACE

The contents of this book, like the content of any course of basic instruction, are offered as a clarification of certain fundamental areas of enquiry and a spur to the young artist to continue for himself a constant inquisitiveness about the phenomena of pictorial and plastic expression. It does not pretend to be more than an introduction to a field that is capable of almost limitless extension, personal variation and individual emphasis. How a student approaches this field of enquiry is less important than the fact of his reaching it. Emphatically this is not a primer in a special sort of art. By now we should have realised that it is too easy to dragoon young students in a certain direction by offering them only a censored part of what should be a comprehensive and undogmatic training – it is as easy and as valueless to create hot-houses for producing pseudo constructivists as it was for producing pseudo impressionists. It may, in fact, be necessary for many a young painter to be in active rebellion against what he finds here, or in any training he receives; it will be for him to prove the validity of his rebellion by his work. Johannes Itten's reply to his students cannot be bettered – 'If you, unknowing, are able to create masterpieces in colour, then unknowledge is your way. But if you are unable to create masterpieces in colour out of your unknowledge, then you ought to look for knowledge.'

Maurice de Sausmarez

plate 2
Child's dress made from two pieces of tracing paper, painted with black ink on the inside and stitched together

CHAPTER 1

INTRODUCTION

Most students, and their teachers, are aware of the fact that changes and developments have taken place in the visual and plastic arts since the beginning of the twentieth century which necessitate revision and extensions in the training of the young artist. We need only think of the significant phases of the development of Painting and Sculpture during the period from Fauvism and Cubism to Mondrian's late work, action-painting and the 'hard-edge' school, or of the changed character of architecture, commercial and industrial design over the same period, to realise that the nature of art and design has been profoundly and permanently affected. Although the majority of the great figures in the Modern Movement received a traditional academic training interpreted in nineteenth-century terms, most of them rebelled against those aspects of training which had become empty, and against criteria largely meaningless in the face of a rapidly changing social and cultural pattern. Debased attenuations of traditional academic teaching placed too little value on looking in order to see and experience, and too much on looking merely to verify the 'facts' of intellectual preconceptions – anatomical, perspectival, botanical; technical method became more important than the power of invention; cultivated solutions of problems more important than personal experiment and free enquiry.

Five factors in particular seem to dominate the changes that have occurred in ideas about creative activity, which must inevitably affect ideas of training. First, a rejection of conventions and an acceptance of the idea that only information which is derived from our own experience can be considered valid for us and for our expressive resources. Second, that information which we gain from an appreciation of the physical nature of our materials and their formal and spatial functioning is as important, if not more important, than information restricted to the visible facts of nature. Third, that a visual art is dependent upon the expressive and constructive use of the specific phenomena of *vision* and that literary or other associations are essentially ancillary. Fourth, that the total personality is involved in making aesthetic decisions and that personal preferences form the inescapable bases of truly individual expression. Fifth, that art is not based on a number of static concepts but changes and extends its boundaries in response to the shifts of emphasis in the

plate 3
Collage of fabric, papers and paint on canvas

plate 4
A drawing made from an assem-
blage of easels, chairs and table in
which an exclusive concern with
dimensions and silhouette shapes
(the space between solids being
represented in black chalk) has
resulted in a dynamic pattern

intellectual and emotional situation of each period in history.

For us, the consequences can be summarised as follows. Our idea of fundamental training needs to develop personal enquiry on the basis of practice, not theory, seeking always the individual solution to each problem. It needs to place emphasis on intuitive and analytical work with materials and formative principles. There must be a primary concern for visual response to what is taking place and decisions will be dependent on this, inevitably influenced by subjective preference arising out of the differences in psychological make-up. Study will reflect the changed character of our present interpretation of some of the fundamental concepts of art and design, of structure and space.

To meet the demand for revision of our attitude to initial training, courses in what has become known as Basic Design have been introduced into many schools of art, but too often, far from assisting the situation, this has frequently created new problems. The difficulty usually arises from the fact that there has been failure to think critically about the nature of these courses, failure to save them from the awful fate of becoming blinkers in which young talents trot docilely to a certain stylistic vacuity, and failure to ensure that they establish effective bridgeheads for contacting and influencing the more specialised provinces of creative activity, painting, sculpture, graphic design etc. Basic design is in danger of creating for itself a frighteningly self-sufficient art-form, a deadly academicism of geometric abstraction for young painters, and for young designers a quick route to the slick sophistications of up-to-the-minute graphic design. The predominantly analytical and dissective methods which have successfully isolated the component factors and elements of pictorial and structural expression have assumed that the processes of expressive creative synthesis would remain undiminished. The assumption has proved false in the majority of cases – a debilitated process of assembling has replaced the urgent pressures of personal statement, taste has succeeded intensity as the arbiter. It is for this reason that some of the earliest enthusiasts of Basic Design have attacked its later manifestations. It cannot be too often reiterated that Basic Design should be:

A an attitude of mind, not a method

B primarily a form of enquiry, not a new art form

C not only an enquiry about the marks and structures which appear out of the materials used, but also an enquiry about the sources and terms of personal expression and reaction to the world around us

D concerned with form in a fundamental sense in every field, it is not exclusively abstract or non-figurative; there is as much need for intensive rethinking and reshaping of our attitude to 'realism' and figural studies

E emphatically not an end in itself but a means of making the individual more acutely aware of the expressive resources at his command; a fostering of an inquisitiveness about phenomena, great and small, on the paper or canvas, in the external world or the interior world of visions, personal reactions and preferences.

Accepting then the role of enquiry about the simplest and most fundamental factors of creative visual experience, we need to start from marks made by tools and materials usually at our disposal, and from the fact of vision itself. A visual art is concerned with marks made to be seen. The marks must be made with an implement and in a material or medium. The implement, be it stick, pen, chalk or

brush, will make marks peculiar to its structure and nature, and the material or medium will demonstrate in sympathetic or antipathetic response according to whether its nature is in accord with the character of the implement used (paint works naturally with a brush – it would work against a pen). An appreciation of the character and nature of these marks is fundamental to any attempt to build truly within the medium. But already it will be noted that there is a different 'pulse-rate' in each mark, an inner dynamic which acts upon the surrounding space. This 'pulse-rate' differs with each individual and arises as a consequence of factors too diffuse and deeply embedded psychologically to be susceptible to analysis. With the merest spot we make contact with the dynamics of visual form and field of subjective response.

Every visual experience is at one and the same time a receiving of fragmentary information, a giving of form to these visual sensations and the arousing of felt response. In what follows we must be careful to remember that, for the artist, what ultimately matters is this quality of feeling which results.

The light signals which bombard the retina are decoded with real clarity over a surprisingly small area at any given moment. The eye can focus upon only a very small area, and to obtain adequate information it quickly moves around the visual field collecting a succession of focused data. After a rapid scanning of the situation in front of us, we as it were stitch together all the received messages and form in our minds a visual image. The action is so fast as to appear instantaneous and yet it calls upon all our previous experience of the world of material form and space. How else can we account for the astonishing fact that the strange shape which the eye *actually* receives when looking at a table-top receding into the distance is immediately understood as implying a square or a rectangle? We do not in fact *see* either of these geometrical figures and yet any deviation in the observed shape is noted and interpreted as a distortion

plate 5

Marks made by tools: pencils, charcoal, sponge, conté, pens, brushes, palette knife, stencil brush

plate 6

A sequence of similar shapes built up horizontally on the same principle as geographical physical contour maps – shapes cut from plywood in this instance and constructed in superimposed layers

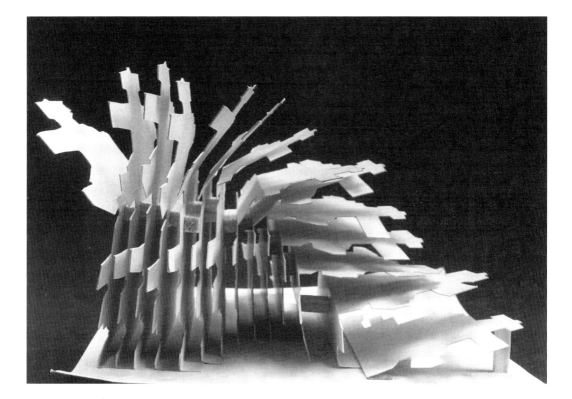

plate 7
Another example of similar shapes repeated in a sequence. Flat card silhouettes were arranged vertically to show movement emerging from a flat sheet into three dimensions

of the square or rectangle. We interpret perception by the application of pre-existing concepts, 'bottle', 'table', 'chair', etc., and we are baffled by visual experience for which we have no ready-made referent, no 'label'. Of course at a much earlier stage the use of colour and reactions to it on the part of very young children in their painting are so diffused and so charged with irrational internal fantasy that this reference to specific external objects and situations is of entirely secondary importance.

For most people beyond the stage of adolescence their early essays in drawing and painting are largely concerned with illustration, making things agree with the labels they have formed in their minds. They are seldom concerned about the force of 'redness' in a red but with the fact that it can effectively describe fire, blood or strawberries. For the artist, not only this but also the behaviour of the forces or energies contained in colours, shapes and lines are of primary importance; and a large part of this book is devoted to a study of these pure dynamic forces in situations where our customary 'labelling' is virtually impossible. Ozenfant has referred to it as 'the geometry of sensation'; this book has the title 'the Dynamics of Visual Form' (dynamics – moving forces; form – mode in which a thing exists or manifests itself – Concise *Oxford Dictionary*. One of the meanings given to the French word *forme* is 'manner of acting

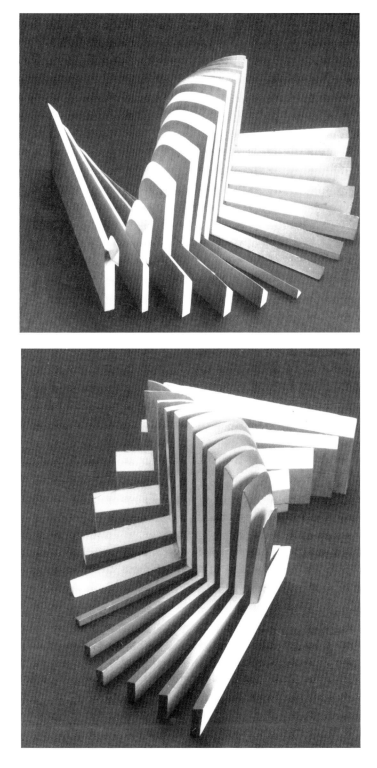

plates 8a & b
In contrast to plates 6 and 7, a
repetitive sequence was here
arrived at by slicing a solid piece
of wood into equal sections and
arranging these to radiate from a
point (seen from two positions)

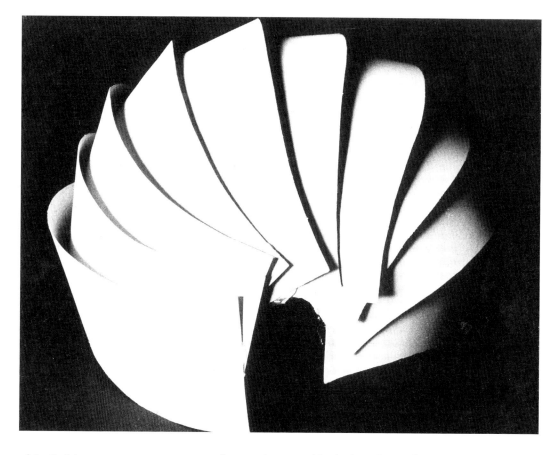

plates 9a & b
Structure made from overlapping
card creating a shell-like form.

or of expressing oneself' which is also to the point). The definition of Form given by an eminent scientist, viz. 'a diagram of forces', perhaps comes closest to the main purpose of this book, which is to examine the rudimentary forces brought into being through graphic marks, dimensional relationships, juxtaposed colours, etc., leaving to the individual's talent and temperament the terms in which he expresses himself. It is the counterpart to mastering the elementary signs of a language (formation and relationship to create coherences), but, by comparison, the primary forces operating in the act of looking provide us with prodigious subtlety and variety. Furthermore visual coherence is more related to our neural and psycho-physiological being than to our processes of intellection. It is for this reason that we cannot describe or define this coherence, we can only acknowledge it when it is experienced through feeling. Optical forces are continuously operative, forces of attraction and repulsion, of expansion and contraction according to the situation of shapes and colours presented to our eyes. As we have already noted, sight is more than the mere optical stimulation of the retina by haphazard light rays, which the mind concurrently organises into spatial

units. It is virtually impossible to perceive units isolated from and unaffected by the context in which they appear. Relationship is inescapable and this makes the act of looking a dynamic experience.

It is vitally important that at every stage in the development discussed in this book, the disciplined considered statement should not exclude the field of free spontaneous gesture, the gesture of direct emotional intensity. Unconscious impulses, much more often than not, are the factors that guide our decisions in working, and it is vitally important that we assist the development of intuitive judgement working with the natural momentum of our feelings. In working, states of feeling are accompanied by a unique sense of a unity of purpose in which the placing of form, of line, of colour is implicit. Nothing must stand in the way of this sense of organic unity and the natural rhythm of working.

To me it seems equally important that initial experience of the primary factors discussed in this book should not be exclusively in 'abstract' geometric terms but should be related directly to personal imagery and, wherever possible, should be translated into three dimensions in the form of constructions. Furthermore, situations in

the external world which demonstrate the dynamic principles under review at each stage should be studied and drawings made, selecting in every case the appropriate factor for emphasis.

It is good training to make drawings of the constructions after they have been made, and occasionally to make drawings first and then attempt to build from the information given in the drawings. It is after all what any good carpenter or cabinet maker does, and it is invaluable in demonstrating inadequacies in structural thinking or its graphic translation.

It has been assumed that many of the readers of this book will have no access to equipped studios for either printmaking or sculpture. The suggestions for practical work in both these fields have excluded aspects and developments dependent on either a printing press or apparatus for metal welding and ambitious processes of that kind.

The student will need sufficient material, and cheap enough, for him never to feel the need for special economy; he must always feel free to scrap much of what is done and make a fresh attempt: the cheapest paper, newsprint, for most of the graphic work, and cartridge or drawing paper for studies in colour; designers' colours, acrylics or oil paint; charcoal, pencils, black ink; rubber solution (cement) and scrap materials.

For printmaking: ordinary brown or plain colour linoleum 3⁄8-in. thick and pieces of hardboard; one or two gouges (V tool and Round gouge) of varied sizes from 1⁄8-in. to 1⁄2-in.; a Stanley or other craft or mat knife is invaluable; a 6-in. and a 3-in. plastic roller in brass frames (printmaker's brayer).

Water-soluble printing inks or oil-based inks, available from most art shops.

Three-dimensional experience and practice has been restricted to materials like cardboard, paper, plywood, wire, dowel-rods, plaster, papier-maché, drinking straws, glue, pins and tacks.

Plaster of Paris, with just enough admixture of PVA to delay the action of setting, or papier-maché can be used over a wire-mesh frame.

Liquid plaster poured into old cardboard boxes or greased biscuit tins will provide blocks for carved forms. Supplies and plasterworking tools can be obtained readily from hardware stores. Although this may appear to be a very limited list of working materials, it is nevertheless adequate for encouraging the mind and sensibilities to conceive and invent spatially.

It should be remembered that this is an Introduction to Basic Studies and for those who want to continue with more sophisticated techniques there is on page 127 – a list of books dealing with various specialised fields; students are advised to consult them as an extension to what is discussed here.

plate 10
Structure made from overlapping scored corrugated cardboard sheets, creating a shell-like form

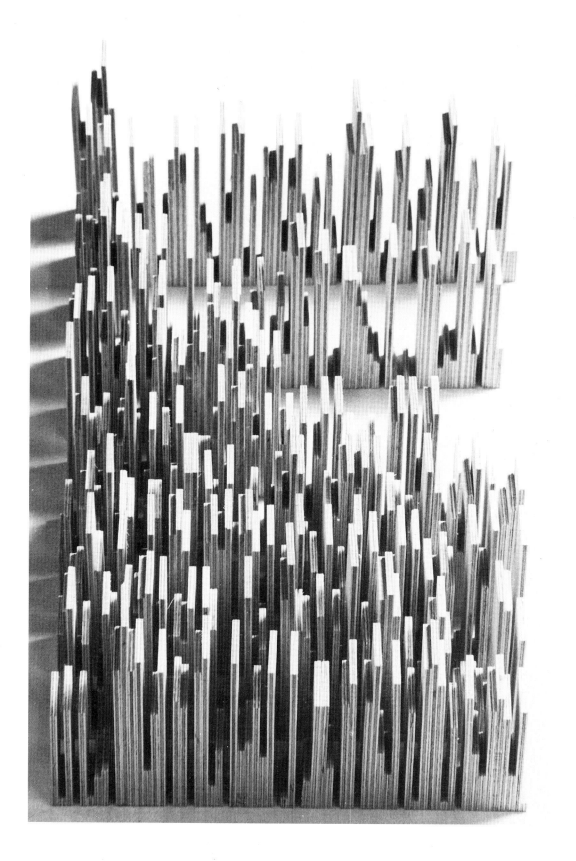

CHAPTER 2

PRIMARY ELEMENTS AND FORCES

The simplest unit, a spot, not only indicates location but is felt to have within itself potential energies of expansion and contraction which activate the surrounding area. When two spots occur there is a statement of measurement and implied direction and the 'inner' energies create a specific tension between them which directly affects the intervening space.

plate 12

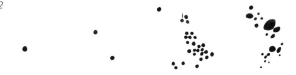

Freely used spots, in clusters or spread out, create a variety of energies and tensions activating the entire area over which they occur. All these sensations are increased if difference in the sizes of the spots is allowed to enter. A line can be thought of as a chain of spots joined together. It indicates position and direction and has within itself a certain energy; the energy appears to travel along its length and to be intensified at either end, speed is implied and the space around it is activated. In a limited way it is capable of expressing emotions, e.g. a thick line is associated with boldness, a straight line with strength and stability, a zig-zag with excitement, although all these are crude generalisations. Straight lines of the same length and thickness in parallel groupings may introduce factors of proportional relationship and rhythmic interval; change the lengths and thicknesses and more complex rhythms and optical 'beat' are experienced.

Horizontal and verticals operating together introduce the principle of balanced oppositions of tensions. The vertical expresses a force which is of primary significance – gravitational pull, the horizontal again contributes a primary sensation – a supporting flatness; the two together produce a deeply satisfying resolved feeling,

plate 11
Rectangular pieces of wood, cut into varying lengths and set out as verticals on a common base, to create an undulating rhythm (see also plate 22)

plate 13

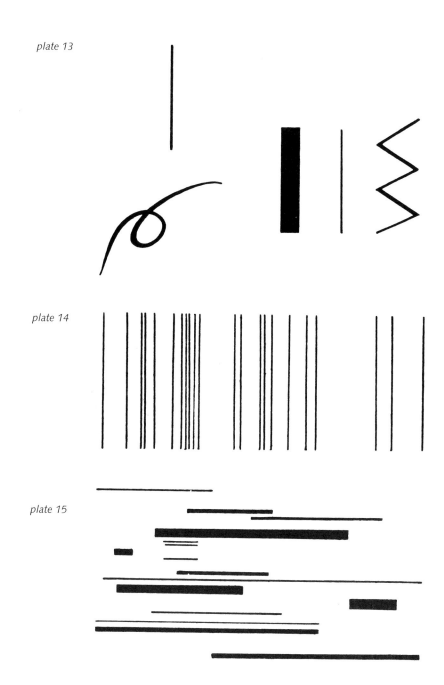

plate 14

plate 15

perhaps because together they symbolise the human experience of absolute balance, of standing erect on level ground.

Diagonals introduce powerful directional impulses, a dynamism which is the outcome of the unresolved tendencies towards vertical and horizontal which are held in balanced suspension (plate 16).

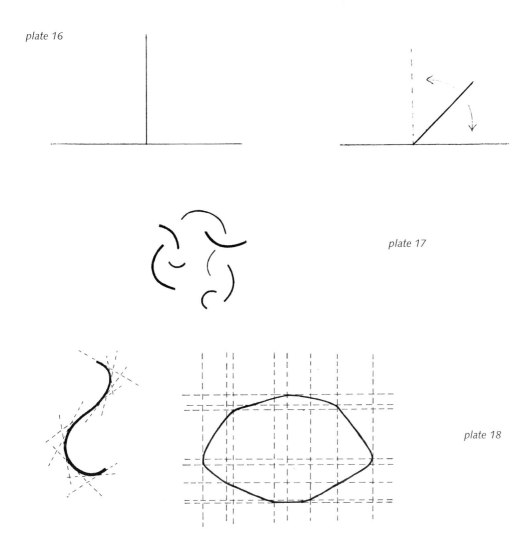

plate 16

plate 17

plate 18

Where line is used in relationships of curves an entirely different rhythmical quality emerges. But it is important to realise that under-lying any curve there exists a framework of rectilinear relationships which explains more simply the directional and proportional factors in the particular curve. And when we are dealing with subtle curved shapes an analysis of these in terms of a vertical-horizontal grid is useful in impressing upon the mind the specific nature of the curva-tures involved. For centuries this has been recommended as a way for the draughtsman to check the particular angles and dimensions and shapes in drawing from nature or from another drawing. (Van Gogh made use of a traditional 'drawing-frame' long after his early days of self training – see letter to his brother Theo, No. 223.) Without perhaps realising it, many a mature artist is referring to a

plate 19
A number of basic elements are selected and the student is then asked to explore as many closely knit inter-relationships as possible. The variety of visual structures from these simple units is immense

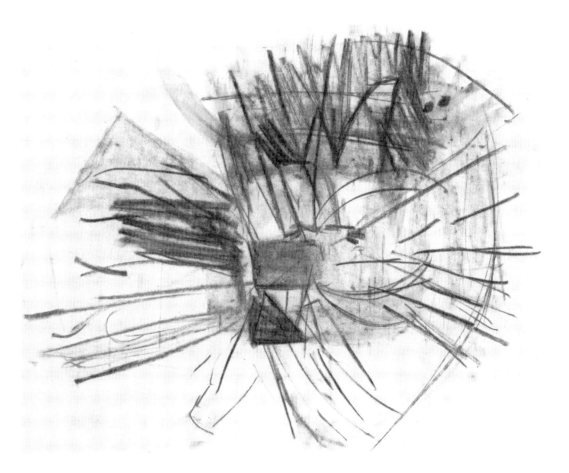

plate 20
A free spontaneous statement
which utilises many of the elements discussed in this chapter

vertical-horizontal constant as he draws. Associating rectilinear and curvilinear marks together, the energies which are created between them can be examined and appreciated. The square, the triangle and the circle are the most fundamental planal figures associated with the linear relationships we have been examining, i.e. vertical-horizontal, diagonal, curvilinear.

It will be appreciated that the ability to estimate dimension and relationship is at the root of objective drawing. To be able to estimate and locate points on a surface precedes the more complex task of estimating and locating points in three-dimensional space.

A well-worn but still useful exercise is to press a number of drawing pins at random into a sheet of soft-board and then make an accurate transcription in a drawing of this specific arrangement of the pin heads. The important thing is to avoid any rough and ready estimate and to search with the greatest attention and continuous adjustment and readjustment of the drawing until a satisfactory transcription is achieved. To join up the drawing pins in position with a white thread will produce shapes which, if your drawing is true,

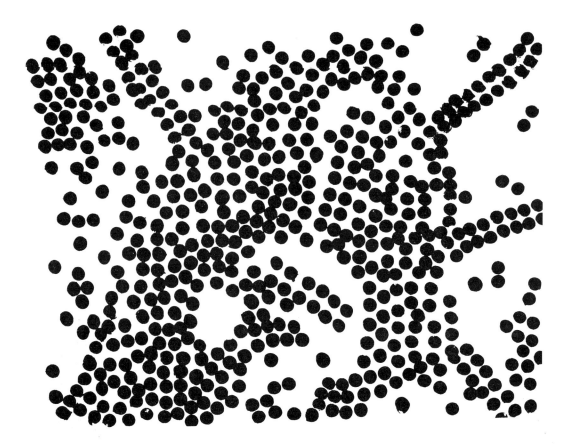

plate 21
One of the elements mentioned in
the next section, a printed dot, is
directly related to personal
imagery. A riot is being quelled by
soldiers – each dot symbolises a
person and the rioters and the soldiers are only distinguished by the
character of the groupings related
to the clear spaces

can be matched by joining the corresponding points in your drawing; the misplacing of any point will result in an incongruous shape.

A considerable number of varied exercises can be devised by
shapes cut out of black or brown paper, and placed on a white sheet
of paper, drinking straws bent in a sequence of lengths and back
upon themselves so as to make straight-lined enclosed shapes; a
length of bent wire pinned onto a board. In each case draw these
on a separate sheet of paper. As much attention must be devoted
to the spaces between the shapes as to the shapes themselves; it has
already been mentioned that in a dynamic visual experience no part
of the visual field is inert or negative. In these objective drawing
exercises the surface plane upon which the pins, the shapes, the
straws, have been placed is put vertically in front of you as you
make your drawing; the transition to three-dimensional estimation
can be achieved by making fresh drawings of these same arrangements with the surface plane placed horizontally so that all the relationships and shapes are now affected by the angle to the eye.

Three-dimensional experience of what has so far been discussed
can best be approached by a similar limitation in the factors to be

considered. Taking any number of rods of the same length and joining them at the ends each time (so that each has the character of a
point in space) build a number of varied structures, e.g. one which
expands in length, one clustered about an implied centre, one
exploiting cubic shapes, one using equilateral triangles.

Take a dowel-rod and cut it into varying lengths; on a cardboard
or plywood base set these out as verticals, first, on a plan of regular
intervals between the rods (this will result in a regular ground plan
but the tops of the rods will create an undulating rhythm in space);
second, on another base set out the verticals in an asymmetrical
way that creates for you satisfying relationships and intervals.

On a base, set up vertically a tall central rod and from this set
out, horizontally, other lengths of rod pushing outwards into space
in varying directions, paying attention to the rhythm of intervals and
lengths and the shape implied by the terminating points. Another
construction might start by sticking together two small sheets of

plate 22

*Rectangular pieces of wood, cut
into varying lengths and set out as
verticals on a common base, to
create an undulating rhythm (see
also plate 11)*

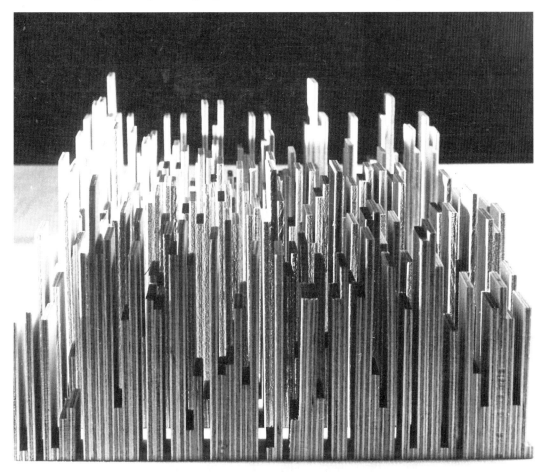

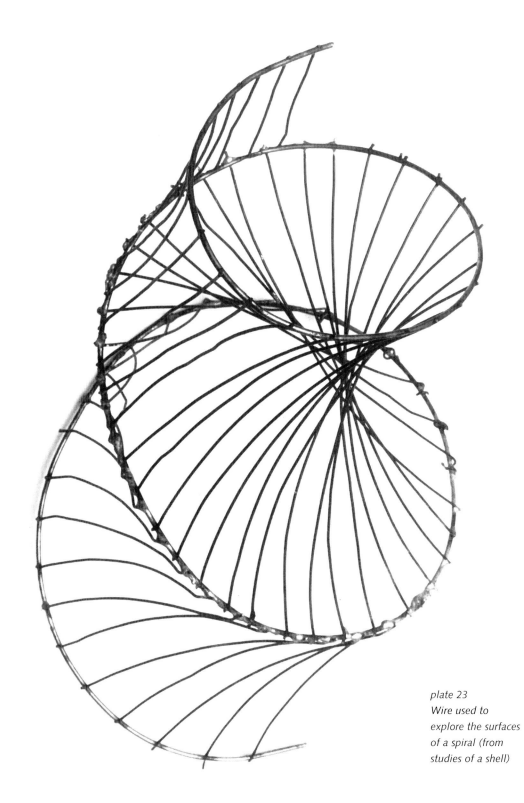

plate 23
Wire used to
explore the surfaces
of a spiral (from
studies of a shell)

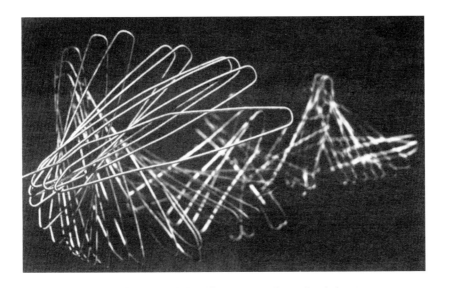

plate 24
Wire rhythmically
extended, based
on a single formal
unit – the long
flattened rectangle
with rounded cor-
ners

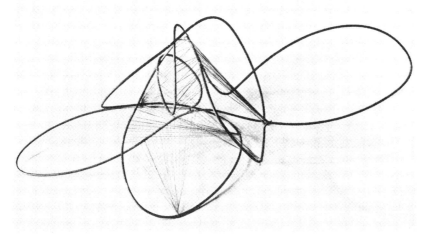

plate 25
Using a wire ring,
a form is arrived
at through twist-
ing: the implied
volume has been
further empha-
sised by the use
of stringing

cardboard at right angles and other similar sheets in pairs stuck at acute angles. These can then be used to construct a vertical 'tower' form or a horizontal articulated form. A continuous length of wire can be bent into a succession of related curves; again the rhythm of intervals and relationships is of prime importance. By making a length of wire into a ring, a form can be arrived at through bending or twisting the ring.

Structures can also be made in card which will assist the development of three-dimensional sensitivity. The simplest forms are reliefs arrived at by cutting the sheet of paper with a knife and folding back the cut pieces (see plate 26 and plates 69 a & b on page 71). Reliefs exploiting the use of vertical and horizontal strips, and of curved forms, can be followed by 'free' structures.

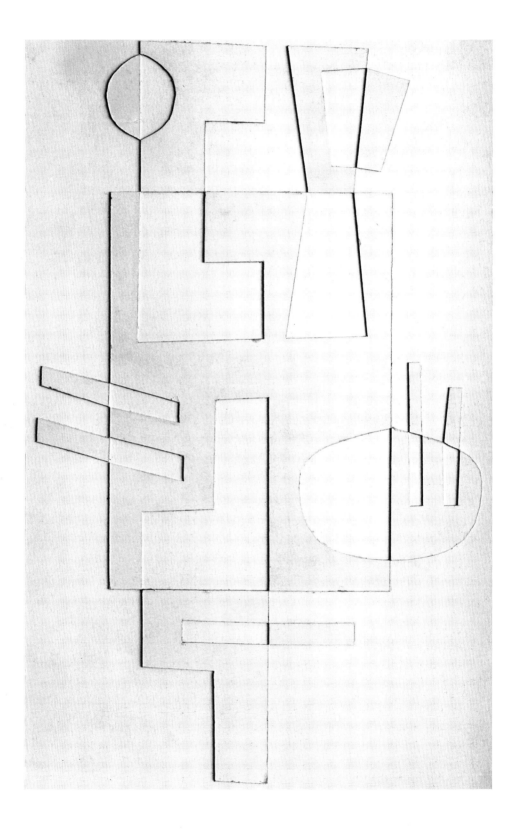

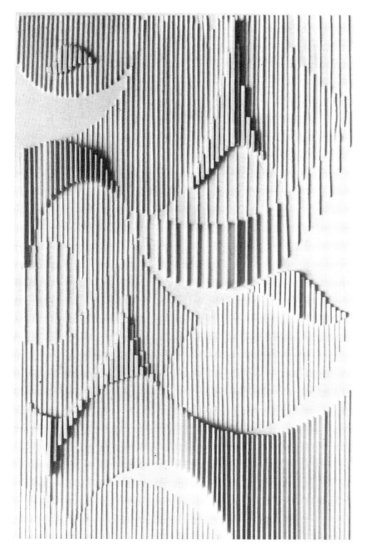

plate 27
Relief using linear units

Light is immensely important in these constructions and should be considered as a fundamental component.

Strips of paper rolled into thin tubes or folded along their length to form right-angle struts can be used to build the constructions, as an alternative to the dowel-rods. (Drinking straws will also be found effective and can be inserted one into the other to extend the length, or bent to produce any angle.)

With clay or plaster simple rectangular or cusplike concavities and convexities, spherical forms, cylindrical columns and cubes can be made singly and then related in ways that appear to increase the inherent energy of each form used.

We soon realise that there is no *absolute* quality or size of shape,

plate 26 (opposite)
Card relief

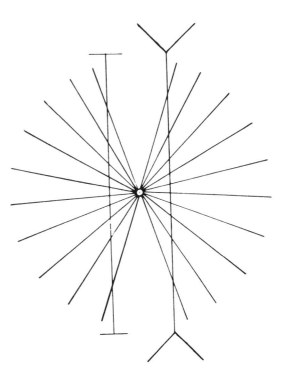

plate 28

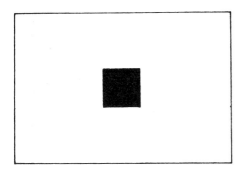

plate 29

colour or brightness, length or breadth because every visual unit is influenced by its optical environment and the inter-relationships which are operating. For example, two parallel lines of exactly equal length look totally different in length and straightness when related (plate 28) to radiating lines and divergent angles. Or change the inter-relationships in plate 29 by changing the optical field (the background) and the visual unit will also appear to change. These dynamic forces operate even within the initial unit itself and this can be demonstrated by turning it about its own centre and contrasting it with other marks.

plate 30
A single unit, a circle, is subjected to 'dynamic' analysis, a differing content of energy appearing in each transformation

Although we may not be aware of it consciously, because we tend to relate what we see to our own bodily reactions to situations in space, shapes appear to fall or be pulled by gravitational factors, appear to lean over, to fly, to move fast or slow, to be trapped, to be free. First exercises should deal with these factors, discovering the differing energies that exist in various simple marks and shapes; followed by an enquiry into the forces which become operative in a variety of groupings, of overlappings, of transparent inter-penetrations. We tend to group units on the basis of proximity or of similarity, i.e. two shapes situated close to each other are seen together as a visual 'whole' even though they may be dissimilar, but more insistent is the linking together of similar units, similar shapes or colours, even though they may be placed far apart from each other in the visual field.

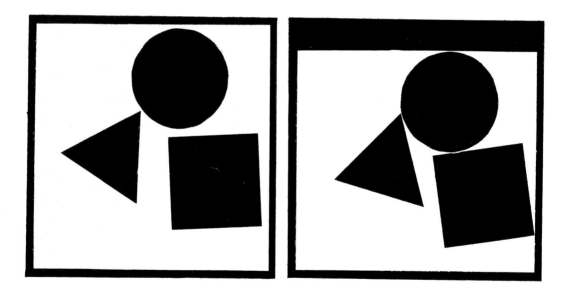

plate 31

The story of contracting space set out strip-cartoonwise. Here we are presented with the felt energies in the forms used, and the unfolding story of their adjustments to pressures demonstrates how readily we identify our human experience of physical space with abstract graphic images

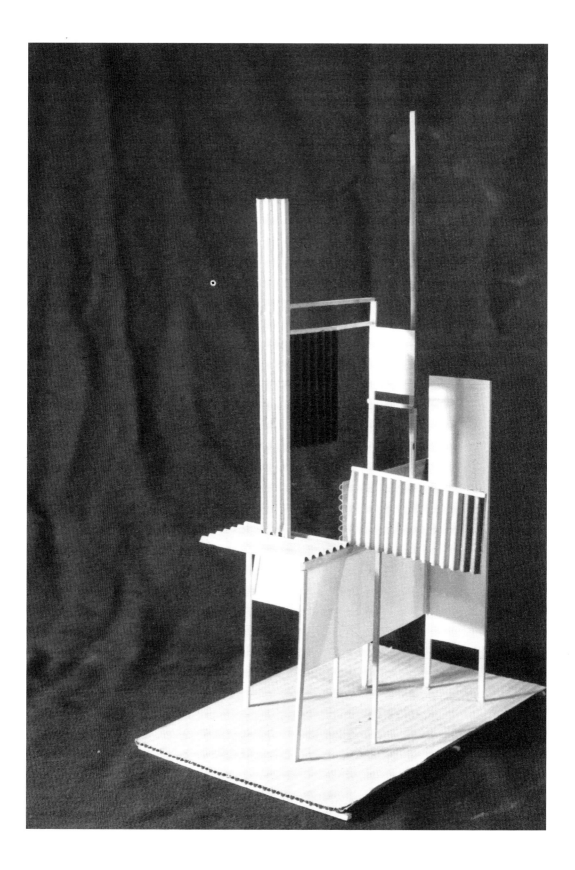

CHAPTER 3

THE TWO-DIMENSIONAL FIELD AND SPACE FRAME

So far we have been concerned only with individual marks and the forces which are brought into play in inter-relating these units. When any mark, the merest dot, is placed on a rectangle of paper, or on a canvas, new forces are brought into being, namely the energies which operate between the mark and the containing sides and corners of the rectangle (plates 33a & b).

And in plate 33a the implied division of the picture area has been indicated by dotted lines. Shift the position of the mark and we arrive at a different area division.

plate 32 (opposite)
A construction of related planes preserving a vertical-horizontal relationship but not contained in an overall enclosing frame

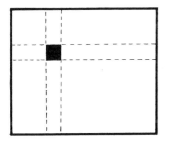
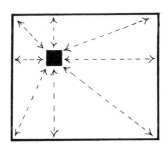

plates 33a & b
Dynamic rectangle

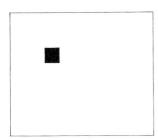
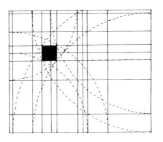

plates 34a & b

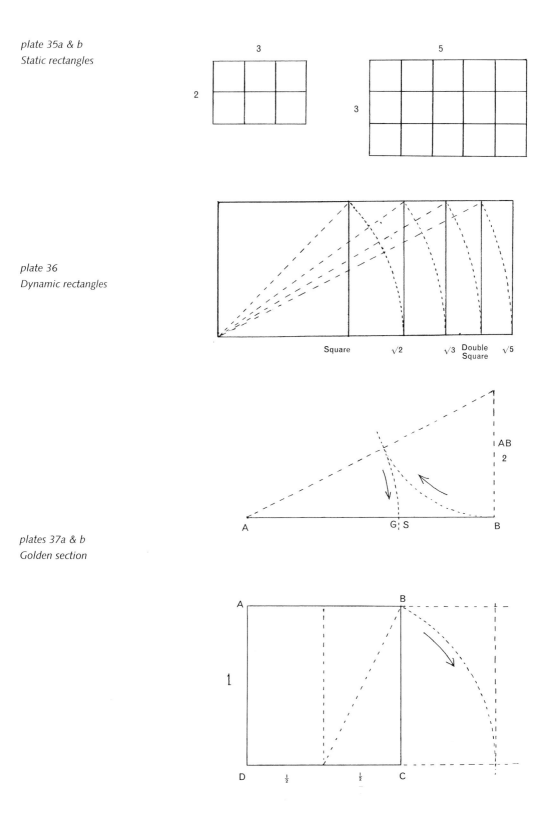

plate 35a & b
Static rectangles

plate 36
Dynamic rectangles

Square   √2   √3   Double   √5
                           Square

plates 37a & b
Golden section

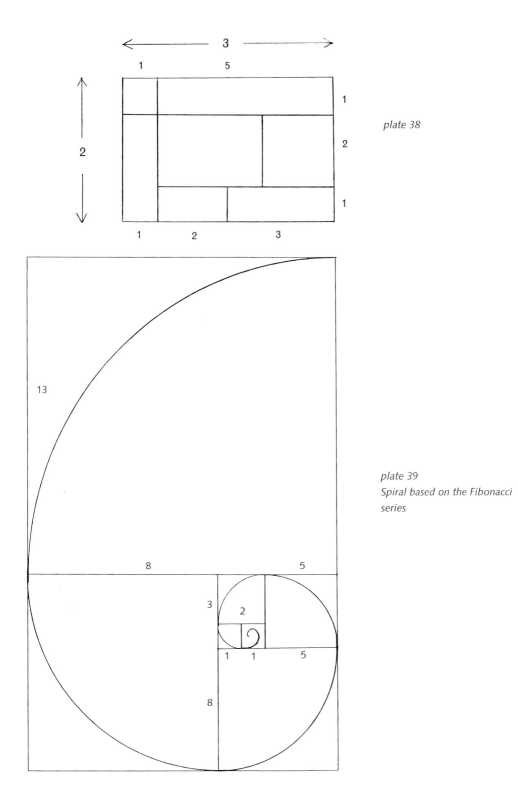

plate 38

plate 39
Spiral based on the Fibonacci
series

plate 40

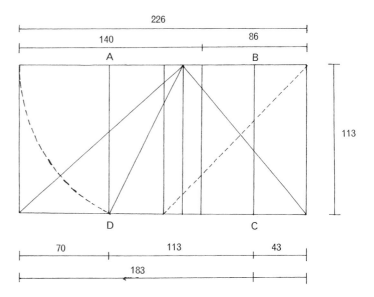

The way in which the picture area is divided is an important issue because it is these fundamental proportions that make the first impact on the eye. The question of proportion has been of continuing interest to artists and at certain periods in the history of painting, in particular the Renaissance and the seventeenth century, geometrical systems of establishing harmonious divisions of the picture area were used, and even of determining the proportions of the picture area itself.

In addition to proportions which used 'simple' numbers 3:2, 4:5, 5:8 and produced *static* rectangles, there were proportions which introduced 'irrational' numbers and produced *dynamic* rectangles √2, √3, √5 which allowed of far more varied treatment in inter-related area division (plates 35a & b and 36). A ratio known as the Golden Section was much used by the Greeks and the artists of the Renaissance and became an established canon of proportion in the later Academies. Its particular distinction lies in the fact that it produces a number of integrally related areas; its character is such that the ratio between the bigger and the smaller measurable quantity is equal to the ratio between the sum of the two and the bigger one (e.g. a line cut in this way results in the total length divided by the larger part being equal to the larger part divided by the smaller part). Plate 37a shows how to divide a line in this ratio; plate 37b) shows how to produce a 'Golden Section' Rectangle. ABCD = a square.

Useful work can be done in analysing some of the great Renaissance masterpieces employing the Golden Section to establish the area divisions.

A related system of expanding relationships comes from the Renaissance – the Fibonacci series; the succeeding number is obtained by adding together the two preceding numbers, i.e. 1, 2,

3, 5, 8...A rectangle divided in this way is shown in plate 38c and the Fibonacci growth pattern spiral in plate 39.

This series was used by Le Corbusier in the development of 'The Modulor'. Plate 40 sets out the principal measures of the modulor. (For a full account see 'The Modulor' by Le Corbusier.)

Plate 34 shows another way of arriving at subdivisions of a rectangle which produce a sense of integration.

In 34(b) every division is arrived at by transferring the primary dimensions established between the initial form and the rectangle.

It will be appreciated that every rectangle can be developed in terms of its area division either systematically on a basis of mathe-

plate 41
A variety of area divisions of a square: a seemingly infinite number of possibilities appear to be present

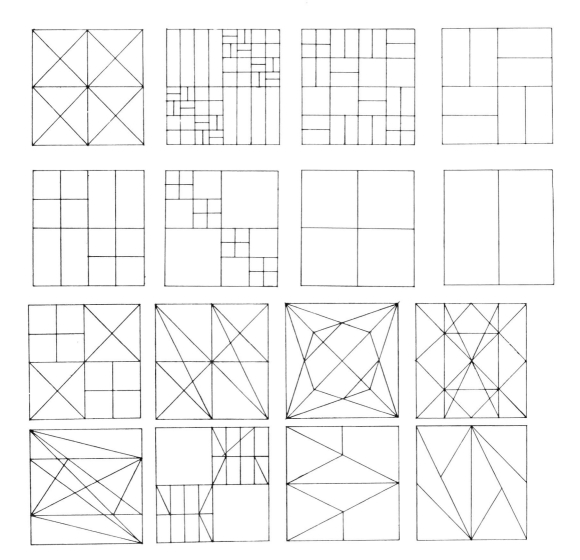

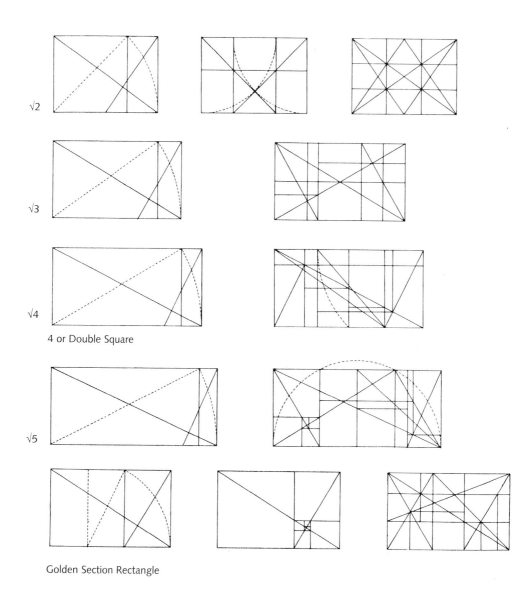

√2

√3

√4

4 or Double Square

√5

Golden Section Rectangle

plate 42
Mathematically established
rectangles and examples of
their possible subdivisions

matical proportion or intuitively, feeling the rightness of the balancing of the parts. Some of the mathematically established rectangles and their subdivisions are set out in plates 41 and 42.

Three-dimensionally this 'area-division' can be studied in the construction of space frames. With dowel-rods, paper tubes or straws, construct a rectangular space, not smaller than 8-in. high and divide it internally into further spaces by vertical and horizontal rods and planes parallel to sides and top; these planes can be of

plate 43
A space frame

paper, cardboard, plywood or perspex according to the nature of the original structure. Carving rectangular spaces into a solid rectangular block of plaster will present the problem in reverse.

Next, thinking in a similar way about the vertical-horizontal planal relationships, make a structure contained in a rectangular space, but without the enclosing rectangular frame – a 'free' construction of thin solid planes and rods. Following this, make a construction still within an implied rectangular space but using a limited number of rectangular solids keeping to the horizontal-vertical principle, with emphasis on size variation and massing. The effect of introducing one diagonally tilted unit can be noted.

A spherical space-frame can be constructed from wire made into

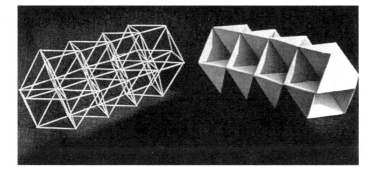

plate 44
'Static' rectangular area-division translated into three-dimensions. The frame is constructed with units of standard length (3-in., cocktail sticks) and the planes applied with cut paper

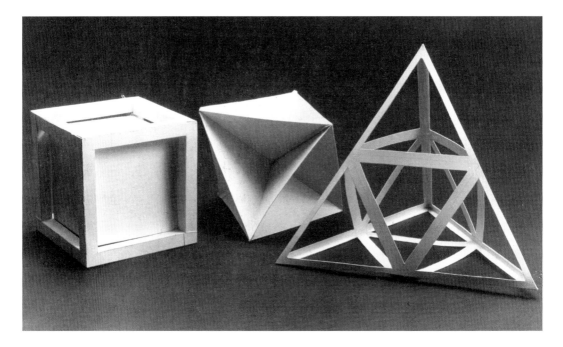

plate 45
Simple geometric forms construct-
ed from the squares and triangles
that are their origins

three rings of equal diameter and these rings fitted one into the other each time at right angles, the space within being subdivided in a similar way to the first rectangular frame previously mentioned; in this case however the containing space-shape should remain spherical.

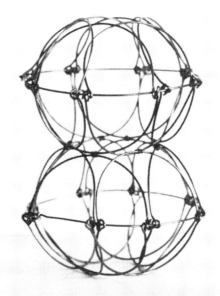

plate 46
A space-frame of wire based on
the idea of two spherical forms
placed one above the other. This
example is in fact an Indian toy –
the wire is attached to the hori-
zontal circular rings in a hooked
way which creates a hinge and
makes the whole structure move-
able

plate 47
An example of intuitive area divi-
sion setting out to achieve an
optical balance limiting the ele-
ments used to rectangles of white,
grey and black (see also plate 51)

A more ambitious structure might attempt to enclose the spherical space-frame within the rectangular one or vice versa. In every case the criterion is not the ingenuity of invention or construction but the satisfying quality of the visually and sensuously balanced relationships.

Intuitive feeling for the subdividing of the rectangle upon which one is working should be strongly developed and is much more likely to be the means adopted by the contemporary painter. A useful way of cultivating this is by taking a number of dissimilar rectangular grounds and limiting oneself to the vertical, horizontal (and later the diagonal), to produce a sequence of subdivided areas which give optically a sense of balance, but a balance which seems to be an equation of dynamic forces (remembering that every unit used is charged with a certain kind of 'energy').

Rectangles of brown paper, newspaper, and one or two coloured papers can be cut and pasted down in relationships that create optically balanced subdivisions.

plate 48
Alternation between figure and ground

CHAPTER 4

SPATIAL FORCES

Look back to plate 33a and 33b; in addition to the tensions which are set up between the mark and the four edges and corners of the picture field, the mark immediately assumes a spatial meaning, and every unit upon it appears to advance or recede from it unless we take steps to 'anchor' the unit on the surface. Spatial forces are thus operative as soon as any mark is seen, and these spatial forces become more apparent as we are able to experience differences amongst the elements which occur in the picture area: differences in (a) the alternation between figure and ground, (b) size, (c) linear relationship, (d) shape, (e) tonal value, (f) colour, (g) texture, (perhaps the most dramatic of these instances is "a").

The sensation of space arising from (a) The alternation between figure and ground

The phenomenon of alternation between figure and ground is often referred to in studies relating to the psychology of perception. In plate 48 (and a number of alternatives can be made by you) spatial ambiguity is experienced, emphatic fluctuations of figure and ground; at one moment the black figure emerges from the white ground, at another the white figure emerges from the black ground. We are forced to recognise the fact that in the field of vision nothing is negative; the space round and in the image is as positive as the image itself. Chinese and Japanese painters have a superb sense of this fact and make the fullest use of it; their calligraphic traditions enforce this concern for the white spaces amongst the brush strokes. Had our own writing traditions continued the thick-thin strokes of the reed pen we ourselves might be more sensitive to the structure of letter images and the positive and negative shapes (see plate 50).

The sensation of space arising from (b) Differences in size

Size almost inevitably introduces the factor of apparent weight, and the distribution of visual weights in achieving an equilibrium is an important matter. But equilibrium must not be confused with pictorial unity – a state of unbalance may often be an essential part of the content to be expressed, yet in such a case a sense of the overall relationship of the visual energies should make it possible to experi-

067261

plate 49
A student using the brush in direct mimicry of an Oriental artist has achieved a similar dynamic in which the white spaces are fully operative

plate 50
(a) White letters on a black background show how the white expands into the border and the letter forms become less obvious, creating an ambiguity of positive and negative shapes

(b) A reversal of (a) but the same effect is not achieved because the black contracts and isolates itself as the positive letter form

(c) By increasing the weight of the black letter forms it becomes possible to arrive at the duality of positive and negative shapes that exists in (a)

ence the picture or design as a whole, rather than as a collection of fragments.

Related to the field of objective drawing, a number of rectangular boxes might be placed on a table top and, in a first drawing, a statement made of all the upright lines as seen by the eye, their lengths being affected by the distance away from the eye; a second drawing selecting for statement all the lines whose apparent direction and length is affected by the angle to the eye, i.e. all lines other than the uprights; a third drawing in which a complete statement is made of the arrangement of forms by drawing each plane separately and exactly as a shape seen by the eye, until all fit to give an account of the solid objects. A similar situation with spherical and

plate 51
Area division, freed from strict rectangulation, exploiting the maximum dynamic by using fragmented components which increase the energies involved

plate 52a (opposite)
A drawing based on the study of
an assemblage of easels, the primary concern being the statement
of intervals and dimensions, the
shapes being reduced to simple
silhouettes

plates 52b & c
Two drawings, similar to plate
52a, by children aged 14–15, also
based on the study of easels

plate 53
A drawing of cubic, cylindrical
and spherical forms on a table top

circular forms, e.g. oranges and plates on a table top, will provide contrasted problems; in this case a first drawing stating the widths of the objects related, a second stating the curvilinear shapes arrived at by drawing the spaces between the solid forms and then adding to this dots or crosses representing the result of an attempt to locate the points in each of the forms nearest to the eye. Remembering the earlier definition of form as 'a diagram of forces', in each drawing the marks or lines made should be appreciated as 'energies' rather than lifeless descriptive 'plottings'. A collection of bottles on a table top provides another opportunity of greater complexity for a series of drawings of this kind. Importance is attached to the practice of first starting by limiting the sort of information to be given, e.g. the disposition of verticals and the height of each, the character of the shapes between the solid forms, and then ending with a drawing which aims at a total statement by a compression of the sort of information searched for in each of the preceding drawings. Progressively more complex forms and collections of forms should be tackled. Each form will be seen to have the appearance of possessing an axial direction or number of changing axial directions (an axial direction being similar to the central core-line in an apple) and these should be sensed and used, either directly or by implication, as a fundamental structural element in any drawing. In fact some drawings should be made in which the sole aim is to state the axial directions implicit in the observed forms. To cultivate the ability to feel oneself at the centre of the form, drawing it as it were from within, is essential. The cultivation of the ability to feel oneself into the centre of the form or structure and the question of axial direction are crucial factors in three-dimensional construction.

To assist the first of these, attempts to build from a centre outwards can be undertaken. For example with spokes or radials of

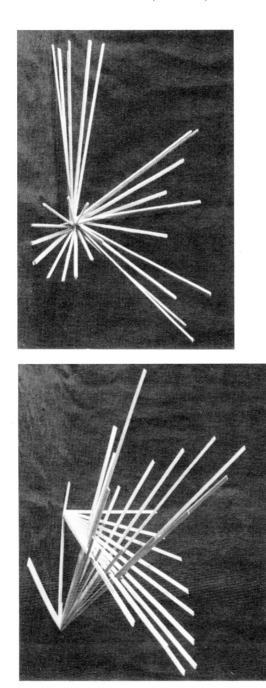

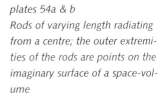

plates 54a & b
Rods of varying length radiating from a centre; the outer extremities of the rods are points on the imaginary surface of a space-volume

plate 55
A rectilinear structure is used as the controlling factor in determining the character of the arcs described by the wire

varying lengths build outwards from one or more linked points in space; the extremities of the spokes will define a space-shape.

Starting with any asymmetrical angular construction of rods, build on it a curved form with wire, the wire being connected to each corner of the initial angular structure (see plate 55).

Changing axial direction might be studied by building a structure of rectangular solids (matchboxes could be used), turning one upon the other and also changing their upward directional thrusts.

A variety of structures might be built on the principle of the continuously changing directions of the inner core of the form (see plate 56).

plate 56
A structure of rectangular solids
on a turning axis

plate 57
Repeated rectangular shapes, cut
and folded from a single flat sheet
of card, extend upwards into
space, continuously changing
direction

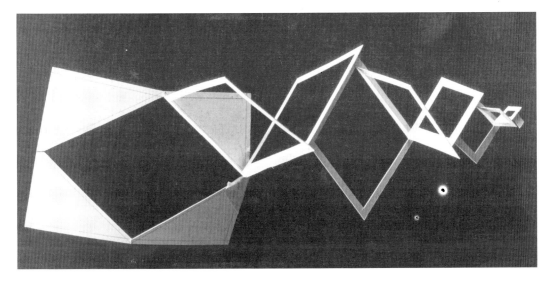

The sensation of space arising from (c) Linear relationships

Since the Renaissance the system of representing natural space by means of the static geometrical system, linear perspective, has been widely known and used. Its value as part of foundational training is questionable, since by offering the student a ready-made recipe for achieving an illusion of space it curbs his spirit of enquiry and he may find himself drawing by academic theory of spatial projection and control rather than from sensation and personal observation. Not only does its logic and operation imply one fixed viewpoint, thereby freezing the entire visual field into static rather than dynamic relationships, but its 'one-eyed' geometry rules out the sense of physi-

plate 58
Linear relationships, freed from the mechanical rule of perspective, creating a space structure

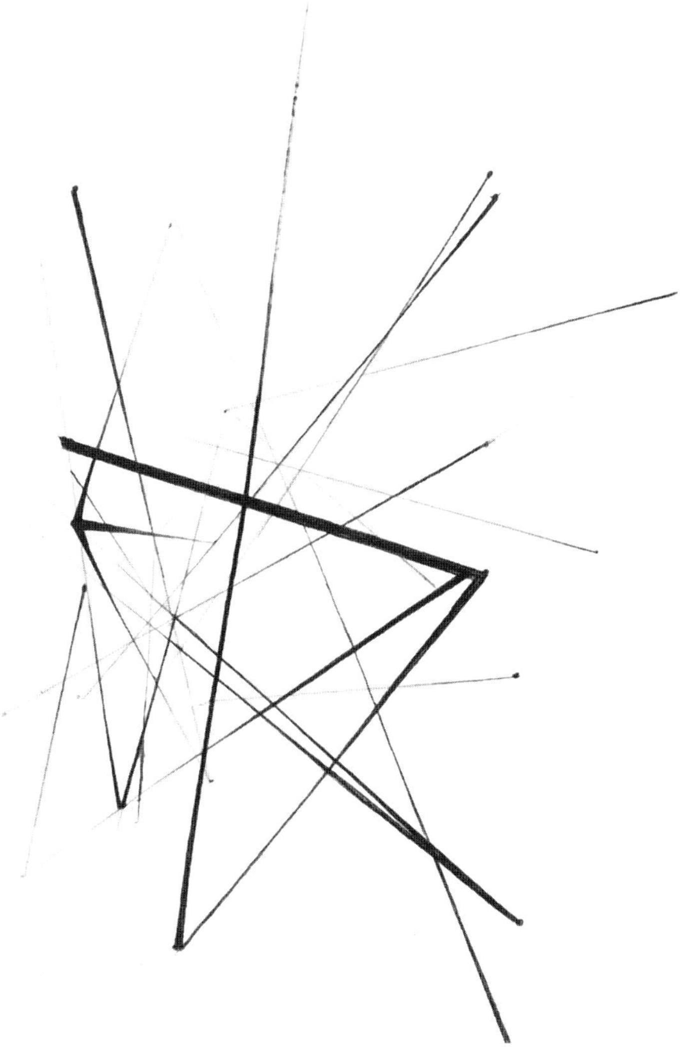

cal involvement, body-felt interpreting of space and forms in space which has previously been described as an essential human concomitant of spatial experience and conception. Few images of a plate could be less true to human vision than the clinical precision of a perfectly constructed elipse.

In order to create a dynamic field of visual relationships many of the earlier masters appear to have used multiple vanishing points and eye levels. Since the beginning of this century, by a rejection of the image as a motionless catalogue of optical facts, the spectator has been made an integral part of the visual image by a sense of his participating in the actions and reactions of the artist as he translates the experience of the total flux of space. This was a central feature of the Futurist manifesto of 1910, and was further exemplified in the work of the school of American action painting.

Linear relationship freed from the mechanical rule of perspective presents us with an immensely varied field of spatial representation. The length of lines, the width of lines, the angles of inclination, the position of lines relative to the outer edges of the picture space, all these factors influence the spatial functioning. Even the picture space itself is charged with a certain dynamic potential by the fact that we are psychologically predisposed to identify the bottom of the picture area with the closest visual material and the top with the most distant.

The sensation of space arising from (d) The exploitation of differences in shape

Rectilinear shapes and curvilinear shapes appear to have differing potentials in terms of suggested movement – in general the latter appear to move more swiftly than the former, though it is possible through changing the linear relationships to increase or decrease the speed. For example, a star shape of a certain kind has as great an apparent speed as almost any curvilinear shape.

In considering all these aspects of space sensation, not only can separate individual units be used, but overlapping and transparent inter-penetrations of units will be seen to increase the range of possibilities.

Constructions in three dimensions should be attempted to accompany the study of all these factors, using the simple materials mentioned earlier. A limitation in materials is perhaps the greatest stimulus to inventiveness. The development of the powers of invention precedes and far exceeds in value the training in technical skills however sophisticated these may be.

The strength of some seemingly fragile constructions if well designed and well constructed is amazing. There is a record of one tower construction 9-in. high with a base 4½-in. square, made of ⅛-in. square-section balsa wood and and balsa cement, carrying

plate 59 (overleaf)
A drawing in which the free use
of a number of vanishing points
and eye levels is implied

2178 times its own weight. Plates 43, 44 and 61 are some examples of what can be achieved with limited materials.

This brings us to another aspect of basic training in drawing; opportunities for cultivating the ability to draw from the evidence purely of touch. It should be possible for a draughtsman to go to a cupboard and, without using his eyes but merely by handling an object, feeling it by touch all over, to make a presentable statement in a drawing of the object from that amount of information. This is no gimmick, it is training in the basic transference of oneself into the substantial presence of a form. Like so much else in the field of drawing it is something that can be strengthened by cultivation, but it is, of course, dependent on an initial sensibility and capacity for deep sensuous experience. In making drawings of this kind it will probably be found that precise definition in the sense of an incisive contour is untrue to the experience; a statement which gradually emerges from a complex of marks, groping for position and relationship, will probably be nearer to the 'felt' image. This is likely to characterise drawings which are based on recollections of forms seen earlier, or of images which emerge from 'imagination' or subcon-

plate 60
Using subtly varied forms derived from the 'families' of the circle and the square, and equal subtlety in the variety of size, this student has created a spatial sensation with a high degree of tension operating between the individual units. This example is almost equally applicable to section (b)

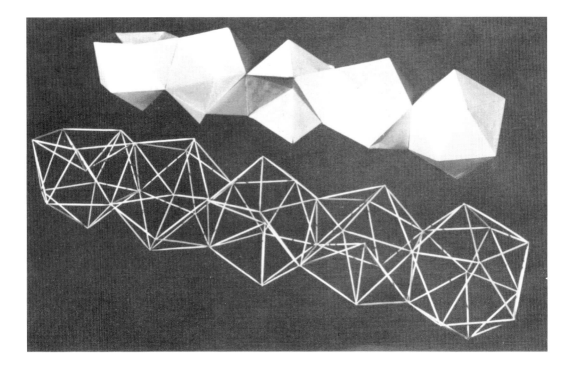

plate 61

A structure made in a similar way to plate 44 (see page 47) but freed from the 'static' grid. The form is conceived as an extending flow of identical geometrical units on a turning axis

scious levels of experience (it is likely but not necessarily so, viz. Blake's clear and brittle line drawings). This may be the appropriate moment for it to be said that no special virtue is attached to any means of drawing or way of drawing. Some students may draw more naturally, i.e. personally, with a matchstick dipped in ink than with a sharpened pencil, some may be temperamentally disposed to expressing themselves through a brittle wiry line, or the rich velvet-like density of impulsively restated estimates of the forms. The imperative factor is that of naturalness, i.e. consistency with the temperament and aim of the artist.

The sensation of space arising from (e) Differences in tonal values

Here again we make contact with a long-established means of creating and controlling space, the factor of tonal value. A tonal scale can most simply be described as a scale measuring degrees of brightness, and if we construct one by forming nine steps from black to white this is about as complex a scale as the eye will distinguish without difficulty, viz. plate 94. By subtle juxtaposing of tones an effective control of space can be established.

The tonal scale that has been constructed may be used to measure the corresponding values of chromatic colours (see plate 94 on page 105) – i.e. any colour may be measured against a grey having the same brightness value. It is more reasonable to speak of 'colour-tones' than to perpetuate an unreal separation of tone (implying impossible colourless greys) from colour.

Light and shadow in a representational picture imply a basic abstraction – the abstraction involving the fixing of what is in a state of flux, i.e. the light source, and the position of the spectator's eyes relative to the object seen. It is possible to push this abstraction further so that it no longer implies a fixed position for the spectator but is used as a convention for explaining the articulation of surfaces (e.g. a cubist 'facet' painting), for organising the broad area-division of the rectangle, for psychological tension in the image, but in all these instances pictorial spatial coherence can only come from an organised use of the tensions between the relative brightness values.

Clearly the three-dimensional field is continuously subject to the influence of light and it is possible, and also helpful, to reverse the situation in which we usually tend to think of the sold structure being revealed by the light. If instead we think of the light as being the element to be fashioned, we can devise planal projections which through the angle of their placing and the extent of their area will act as light modulators. Constructions can be made from flat sheets of stiff paper in which the forms or shapes are cut and folded for-

plate 62
A still-life worked out in simple areas of tone

plate 63
A paper relief construction made by cutting shapes in the stiff paper and folding them forward at the required angle to receive the amount of light intended and consequently to control the extent and character of the cast shadow

plate 64
A paper relief constructed in the same way as in plate 63 with the intention of it acting as a light modulator

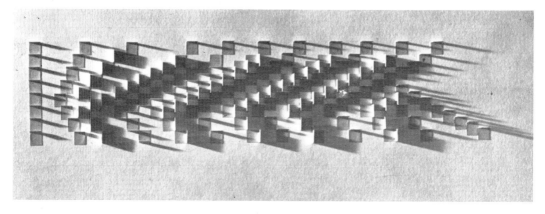

ward so that their angle of inclination to the source of light will control the shape and size and direction of the shadow cast. It will be found that by working within a strictly limited 'family' of shapes on any one construction, and by making full use of the element of rhythmical pattern through repetition, the results will be more powerful than by seeking for perpetual variety and contrast.

The sensation of space arising from (f) Differences in colour

The spatial implication of juxtaposed colours, although it needs to be mentioned here as a means of creating space, must be left for detailed consideration until the field of colour is more fully discussed in Chapter 8.

*plates 65a & b
Forms originating from a
simple 'steps'
theme, painted
black and white
to emphasise
the tonal
contrast, and
arranged in a
repeating
pattern*

plate 66 (opposite)
A sheet of card cut, scored and bent to form a relief producing varied light modulations and tonal pattern effects

plate 67
Light study with modulor design (a construction in thin card)

The sensation of space arising from (g) Differences in texture

This field of visual reaction cannot, of course, be separated from the sense of physical response, the sense of touch. 'Rubbings' of various surfaces can be made, and assembled as 'collages'. A collage is an assemblage of materials which have been stuck together to form a new structure or image (French *coller* = to stick). The original collages were of paper stuck down on a surface, but more recently the term has been stretched to cover any sort of material and a much more extended range of adhesives and means of fixings.

An appreciation of the fact that these rubbings involve the same principle as relief printing, i.e. printing from a raised surface, is an appropriate moment to introduce elementary printmaking.

plate 68
The back of an old zinc litho plate has been used for this experiment in etching. (It is assumed that the student has no special equipment or press.) 'Stopping-out' varnish, soap, wax or strongly adhesive grease is used to make shapes which can be drawn into with a matchstick or other means used for revealing the bare metal. The back of the plate is then coated with a protective covering of the varnish and placed in a porcelain tray (a photographer's developing dish) and a 30% solution of nitric acid and water poured on the drawn surface of the zinc. Take care in handling the acid and keep your head away from the fumes. Twenty to thirty minutes of this 'biting' will be sufficient to produce in relief the shapes protected by the coating of grease etc. Remove the varnish with turps and clean the plate. Ink it up with the roller and take a print

plates 69a & b (opposite)
plate 69a: The card relief, plate 26 on page 34, inked up with a roller
plate 69b: A print taken from plate 69a

plates 70a & b (pages 72 & 73)
Scraps of material of varied texture assembled as a collage. The collage is rolled up with ink and a print taken. Here the collage and the resulting printing are shown side by side

Collections of scraps of material, leaves, etc. exhibiting varied textured surfaces can be assembled as 'blocks' and prints taken from them. The inking up of these collage blocks calls for a soft roller that will adequately spread the ink over the very uneven surface. Constructions of paper, like those which were made as light modulators referred to earlier, can be made and the cut shapes folded right forward and pasted down to the front surface to form a paper-relief. These can be inked up with a roller and prints taken.

Having appreciated that fact that it is the principle of projected surface and variety of texture of the surfaces that operates in this aspect of printmaking, other materials can be used to extend the range of experience. Plain brown lino and hardboard (Masonite) can be cut into with gouges and prints taken from the resulting blocks. By using a fresh piece for each colour and printing one colour over

plates 71a & b
Collages of paint, paper and bub-
blewrap.

plate 72 (opposite)
A collage of old rags. New
beauties of colour are brought
into being through their juxta-
positions and from the strong
textural relationships

another, this elementary printmaking can be extended to encompass simple colour printing.

Collage is a means of revealing unexpected relationships and qualities in materials by placing them in entirely new contexts. In the superb works of Kurt Schwitters fragments of railway tickets, tobacco labels, and what the busy world discards as rubbish, are transformed by their juxtapositions into things of exquisite beauty. Similarly in the works of Burri, bits of old sacks and refuse metal are changed into images of fiercely disturbing intensity. This process of transmutation is at the very centre of artistic creation. What else is the painter or the poet doing but magically endowing the patches of paint and the sounds of words with totally new intensities and overtones of meaning? (See plates 70a and 72.)

Constructions made with junk of all kinds should be attempted – bits of wood, old tins, metal grating, chicken wire, etc., held together by glueing, nailing, sewing, etc. Relief constructions and free-standing constructions can be made and, if it seems appropriate, painted with ordinary house-paint. Attempt to endow each of these constructions with a 'presence', a sense of an underlying 'mood', an intensity that is a product of this specific coming together of the component elements. Do not attempt to achieve this by any means other than the dynamic of the relationships.

plate 73
Variations on a
theme created
by collages of
fabrics each
printed with
some black,
orange and
brown, and then
modified with
the addition of
different papers

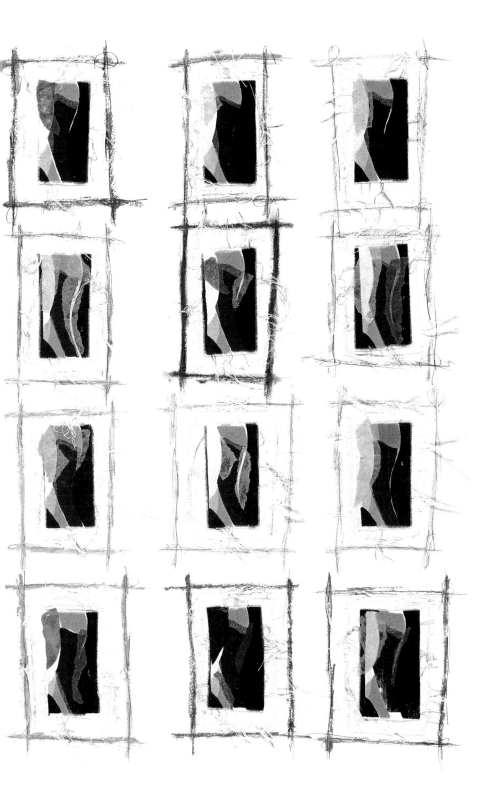

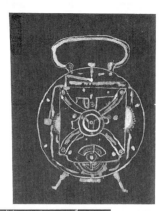

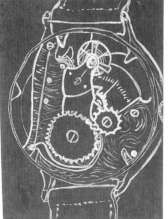

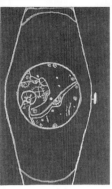
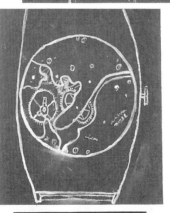
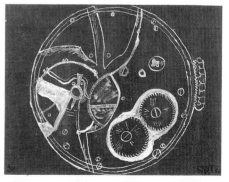

CHAPTER 5

ANALYTICAL DRAWING

Early in this book, it was suggested that any serious attempt to refashion the foundational studies of the young artist today should not only concern itself with the field of pictorial geometry in abstract terms, but should also explore in a fresh way the geometry related to the representation of the visible world. By this I do not mean simply the free reference to external reality as an infinite storehouse of images and 'motifs' which can feed the interior personal world of fantasy, though this is an immense part of its importance to the artist. At this stage I mean something no less exciting and equally revealing: an enquiry into the nature and structure of what we see.

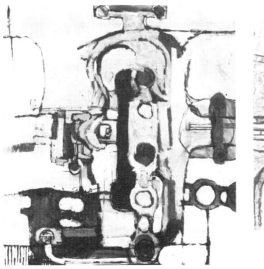

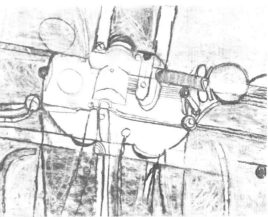

plates 75a & b
Drawings of parts of machinery

It is often assumed that seeing is an activity so instinctive that drawing from direct observation is something we need hardly consider. Nothing could be less helpful. Firstly, it is not easy to see and few people give sufficient time to the intensive, questioning looking that is necessary to cultivate the ability to see. The actual appearance of things is essentially different from the quick pre-conditioned glance of recognition that serves the purposes of every-day living. Secondly, our sense of space and structural coherence is derived

plate 74 (opposite)
A collection of drawings by children aged 13–14 of watch and clock mechanisms

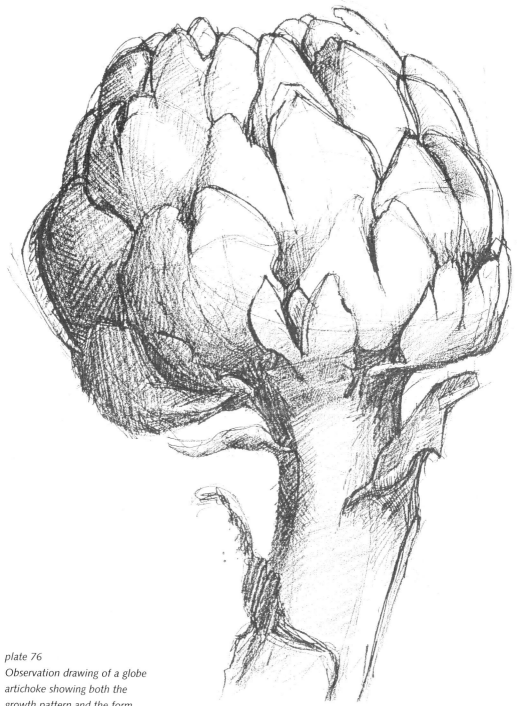

plate 76
*Observation drawing of a globe
artichoke showing both the
growth pattern and the form*

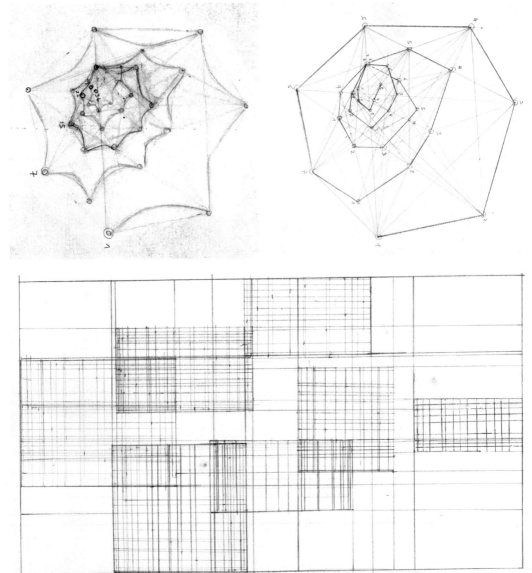

from our experience of the world of physical objects; if we impoverish this sense by failure to explore this objective reality adequately, i.e. intellectually and sensuously, we shall find the work we produce becoming thin and limited. Thirdly, the attempt to be scrupulously true to our sensations of space and colour and structure not only assists us in knowing ourselves but strengthens our powers of independent judgement.

Training the eye to appreciate and assess relationships is a basic necessity – the character of any shape is revealed by a consciousness

plates 77a & b
Above
(a) measured analysis of a shell to arrive at the fundamental geometry and rhythm
(b) a stem and leaves analysed in terms of widths and lengths, the measurements being set out in the form of a grid

plate 78a
In order to clarify and make more
intense the solid structure of the
nude form, lines were drawn on
the model representing the outer-
contours of sections through the
form. The student was encouraged
to continue to imagine these sec-
tions through the form as the
drawing developed

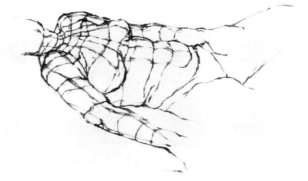

of the relation of its height to its width, of the disposition in space
the critical points of change in its contour.

In addition to the indications for training in objective drawing
that have already been given, drawing which explores the field of
functional forms is of importance. Artists of earlier centuries often
applied themselves to the study of anatomy and architectural drawing; today, not only the inner structure of natural forms (including

microscopic and telescopic images) excites our interest but also the superb functional logic of machinery and man-made forms. Not only is the structural sense strengthened but the powers of formal invention, of design, are stimulated. Cézanne in the nineteenth century, said 'Art is a construction parallel to Nature'; some twentieth-century artists have implied that it may also be 'a construction

plate 78b
Measured drawing of a figure
relating surrounding space, eye-
level and perspective

parallel to Science'. But the artist's interest in the phenomena of 'the machine age' is not an interest in their material functioning but in the visual logic of their relationships or in their symbolic potency, the fact that these visual experiences call up deeper 'personal' images of equivalent power and inter-relatedness. Not only sections cut through natural forms (fruit, vegetables, bulbs, bones, stones), but also parts of bicycles, combustion engines, watch-movements, mincing machines, might be drawn.

Reference has already been made to the sort of analytical drawing encouraged by Kandinsky, an analysis in terms of the lines of inner forces or axial directions; there is also the type of analytical drawing represented by Mondrian's drawings and paintings of church facades and trees of 1909–1914 where a dual process of simplification operates. The first process aims at the elimination of details and the strengthening of the structural movements to be discovered in the object seen, the second aims at representing in equivalent geometric terms the structural principle or law of growth and balance which is formed in the mind by a contemplation of the object. Equally well, other selected aspects of the object (the ground plan of the forms in space, a statement of the extreme limiting points of the forms, the shapes of the lights, statements purely of dimensions) or of graphic interests can serve as principles of analysis; the important thing being the sustained and consistent way in which one particular principle pervades each study, in other words never losing sight of the particular end served by the analysis.

plate 79
A more intuitive approach to the drawing of a figure, related to surrounding space

CHAPTER 6

VISUAL KINETICS

As we have already seen, every spot and every line has energy, and by associating these energies together a visual kinetic is created. Rhythm is the most fundamental aspect of this and the 'visual-beat' of spots and parallel lines, vertical or horizontal, set out with differing intervals between them is a simple example of rhythm changes (see pp. 25–6).

There is no culture which has not conceived of the idea of rhythm in one form or another because rhythm is fundamental to organic growth. It can be the regular repetitive rhythm of simple pattern-making or the rhythm of movement and counter-movement in

plate 81a
Linear dynamic forces

plate 80 (opposite)
A repeated shape, cut from thin card and joined in a spiralling sequence, conveying the sensation of a whirlpool

plate 81b
A few examples of the sort
of linear dynamic forces
referred to in the text. It is
the principle of the dynamic
seen to be operating that
matters, not the individual
instance

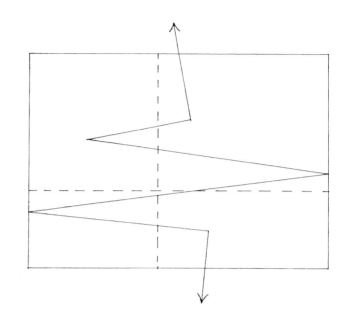

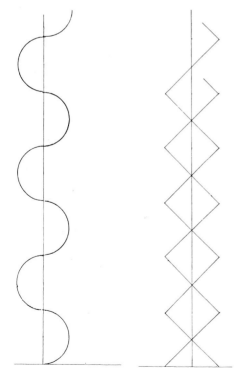

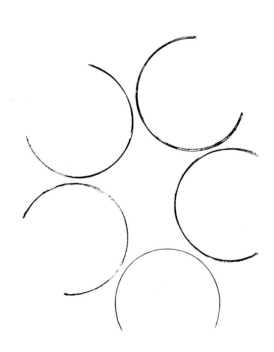

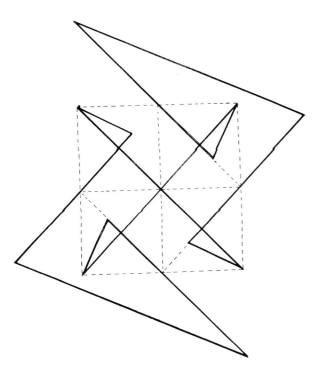

plate 81c
Further examples of linear
dynamic forces

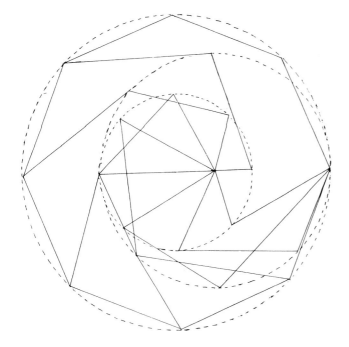

plate 82
Optical sensation of movement
created by a sequence of rhythmic
realignments about a centre which
retains the stability of the original
ground

freely balanced tension. (The simplest form of movement/counter-movement is the pendulum which establishes a balanced tension of forces through the line of gravity.)

We can imagine the same principle of one energy being countered by another extending throughout the entire visual field (e.g. linear thrust and counter-thrust; free movements of curves; spirals; rotation based on circles with a variety of shifted centres; movement in four main directions, upwards and downwards and from side to side).

The forces operating can be likened to those of the pull of gravity, the swing of a pendulum, the opposing forces of pulleys, the principle of buttressing and of levers, the principle of the spring and of the screw, the turning of cogwheels – all these from the fields of nature and technology have their equivalence in the visual arts. The exploration of the field of visual dynamics including the phenomena of so-called 'optical illusion' (what is optical reality if what we see and experience is illusion?) has been a major concern in contemporary art; with some artists it has become a vital and valid means of expression.

Kandinsky's course of analytical drawing was concerned with the extraction of inner lines of force from the complex of forms presented; the objects were considered as energy-tensions and the composition reduced to an arrangement of lines expressing these tensions. The eye is very readily forced into pursuit of a linear direction and, as it follows the line, attributes to it the quality of movement. Such energy-tensions operate also in the 'visual pull' of masses and colours, and movement is achieved by deflecting the eye from concentration at any one point.

Among the Old Masters, Rembrandt's drawings in particular are full of clear examples of energy-tensions in mass and line.

We tend to see and interpret by reference to the stable norm of gravitation so that whenever an object or form is placed in contradiction to the horizontal-vertical axis it seems to imply movement.

Every configuration carries in its own nature an account of the forces, the speed, the actions which created it; every line has an innate kinetic quality independent of its representational content, an essential part of its expressive content being the fact that it is the visible path of the creative act. It is this, added to the belief in 'significant' forms arising from a deeper stratum than consciousness can reach, that has led many modern artists to use techniques which are as free as possible from the obstacles of deliberation, which allow a free flow of organic image formation. Movement in such cases may often be the visible recording of the physical actions of the artist rather than the movement generated by the inner 'energies' of the shapes, colours, etc.

In the previous references to objective drawing it has been assumed that the draughtsman's concern is with the static object. What possibilities are presented if form in movement is accepted, either the draughtsman moving around the objects or the objects moving around the draughtsman? Here too he will be concerned with diagrams of forces, in most cases forces which are intuitively felt to be present in the changing sequences of the movement. If one sets a three-dimensional form in motion and one notes in a drawing fragments of the significant 'phases' of the movement, a new image, a synthetic image compounded of these fragments of retained information, emerges.

We realise, if we have not done so before, that 'a crowd' is not represented by an assembling of individually studied figures but has

plate 83
Utilising the linear dynamic based on the contradiction to the horizontal-vertical axis mentioned in the text, this example represents the force of a wind beating against strong tubular constructed grasses

plate 84
Construction based on the repetition of one unit turned in space to create a visual dynamic

its own lines of rhythm and principles of structure in which the figures are transformed into a sort of malleable substance out of which the total crowd-form is fashioned.

One phase of Cubist analytical drawing is reputed to have been an attempt at a synthesis of different aspects of the forms represented into one compounded image (a sort of moving round the object), not merely aspects ordinarily associated with the 'seen' form but also aspects of the 'known' form (e.g. plan, section, stereometric equivalent, etc). How deliberate this method was is arguable but the drawings themselves clearly suggest this as a possible aim.

An interest in 'dynamism' characterised that whole period, the Futurists attempting drawings which would be virtually diagrams of the 'felt' energies in the passage of a moving form. It is utterly wrong to ascribe to them nothing more than a banal variant of cinematography. Severini, their ablest spokesman, writes 'Movement becomes what it is in reality, a continuity, a synthesis of matter and energy. This aesthetic reality is indefinable and infinite – it neither belongs integrally to the reality of vision nor that of knowledge but participates in both.' He suggests that the symbolising of form in movement is the outcome of the complex influences of vision, of

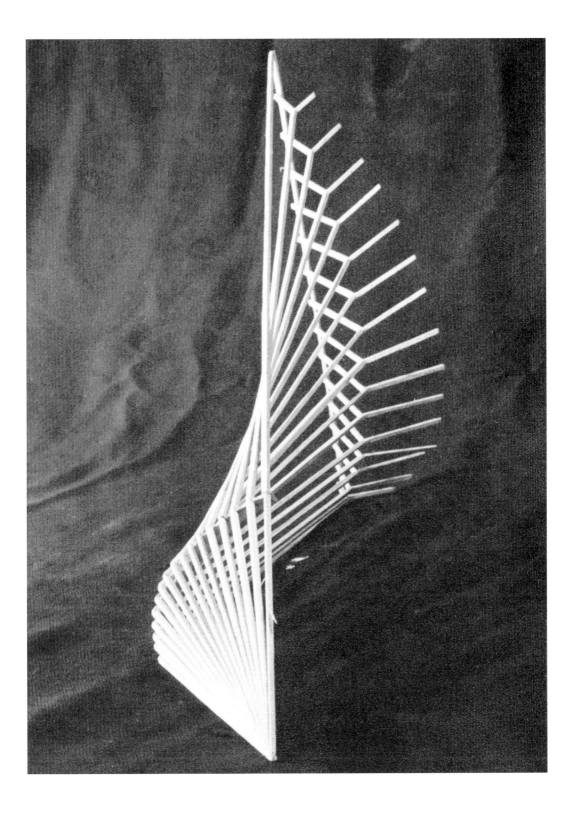

plate 85
Waterproof ink
splattered and
blown on wet
paper. In contrast
to plate 83, the
medium has been
allowed its own
free movement
and the image is
created by chance

plate 86
An image com-
pounded from
fragments selected
intuitively and at
speed from the
sequence of 'phases'
of a moving nude
figure

plate 87 (opposite)
A drawing of a nude figure walking slowly backwards and forwards, made up
from a series of over-lapping images, to create a feeling of movement in space

plate 88
Two experiments in visual kinetics
made by the painter William
Culbert

(a) A photograph of the 'Discus
Thrower' (Discobolus c. 450 BC) is
cut into vertical strips and
reversed so that right-hand forms
in the original are placed on the
left and the original left-hand
forms conclude the movement on
the right. These strips are arranged
so that white intervals between
the strips act as a rhythmic 'flick-
er', creating the sense of movement in the image

memory, of emotion and what he calls 'ambience', the sense of totality which we experience including smells, sounds and other sensations, all of which he believes can be expressed plastically.

New territory seems to be opened up for the draughtsman by this encompassing of all sensational experience. Drawings should be made by accumulating marks made as instantaneous reactions to the experience of watching figures moving about; the marks which should be made at speed and without deliberation should, never-theless, be genuine attempts to grasp a fragment of contour, a directional movement, a point of pivotal emphasis, a 'felt' mass, the rise and fall of shapes, the intuited flow.

Drawings of this kind might be made from a figure moving slow-ly through a limited sequence of actions, continually returning to the original position and going through the same sequence of move-ments. Ten or fifteen minutes of rapid notation, no conscious attempt being made to make the marks fit a preconceived image, striving all the time to become totally involved in the experience of the moving forms. If a model or another figure is not available make drawings in a mirror of yourself in movement. Drawings made of a

figure or objects seen from one position might have, superimposed upon them, imagined statements of what would be seen from the side and from the back. Only after having made your imagined statement should you move round to check how strong your constructive imagination has been. When watching a crowd or being part of a crowd try, by making graphic marks, to get the sense of totality and rhythmic movement of the mass.

Some drawings should be made at so close a distance from a moving figure that it is impossible to focus on a complete form, such as an arm or leg, and only the sense of moving mass of flesh or cloth is experienced.

(b) A 'still' of a dancer cut into small squares and reassembled on the principle of 'reversal', turning each square through 180°

plate 89

The counterpart to plate 86 but here the new images arise out of the fragmentation of the known letter-units and their intuitive reassembling to produce a strongly kinetic effect

In the sphere of three-dimensional structures the mobiles of Calder and early Chadwick would seem to offer suggestions for development, and yet I am doubtful whether it is this construction of mechanisms for *actual* movement that is the most valuable and most basic experience sculpturally. It would seem to me that the translation and embodiment of the sense of movement into material that is itself static is the subtler and more considerable achievement. To attempt a sequence of relationships of curved rhythms, alternating concave and convex forms, moving through a series of quickly changing axial directions, or to construct a form which has the sense of spinning on a central axis, these and other similar studies involving the sense of paths of movement and forms in the process of change would seem to be relevant.

plate 90
A construction of paper utilising
the dynamic of the spiral

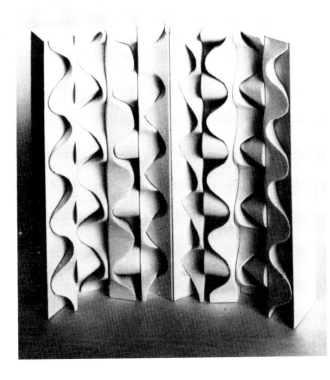

plate 91
A machine-formed relief evoking
a strong sensation of movement in
all dimensions

CHAPTER 7

COLOUR
FUNDAMENTAL STUDIES AND 'OBJECTIVE' PRINCIPLES

Colour is usually considered to be such an intimately subjective field of experience that there may seem little that can be studied on the basis of objective principles. Yet, rightly understood, nothing in this book expounds general rules to be followed – it is only an encouragement to question and explore our sensational responses to basic pictorial phenomena; from this we can ultimately strengthen our subjective opinions and work with greater understanding of the creative potential in our materials.

Often the study of colour is confused for the art student by a failure to distinguish the limits of his special concern. The physicist's interest is in the phenomena of light, the mixing of chromatic light, the classification of colour through an understanding of frequencies and wave lengths of coloured light rays, and touches only peripherally the province of the painter and designer. The physiologist's investigation is of our visual apparatus and the neural reaction to light and colours, and is closer to our interests; the psychologist's interest is in perception and the influence of colour in terms of subjective symbolism, and is even nearer to the centre of our studies, in fact it frequently overlaps. It still remains however to disentangle the artist from these fields in order to discover his specific concern.

His interest can be considered to centre mainly on

A the constructive aspect of colour, i.e. how colour functions in a variety of relationships, and

B the expressive aspect of colour, i.e. its potentiality in translating the visual impression he has of the external world, and its potentiality as an emotionally expressive vehicle for the interior world of symbolic imagery. But these subdivisions are theoretical only and in practice there is perpetual coalescence, emphasis deriving from each artist's temperament.

plate 92
Painting in three layers creating a strong illusion of space and depth - each layer almost a painting in itself.

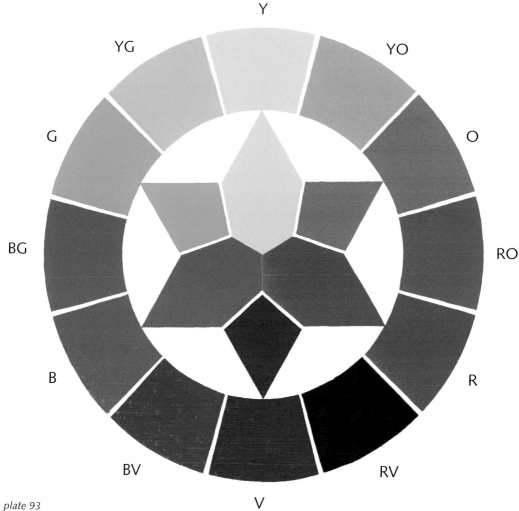

plate 93
The colour-wheel

Colour sensation can be differentiated into four essential characteristics:

1 **Hue** – the quality which distinguishes one colour from another, e.g. orange from red
2 **Tone** – the quality of brightness, i.e. light or dark
3 **Chroma** –the quality of saturation or measure of the colour intensity, e.g. spectral hues are of maximum saturation
4 **Temperature** -the quality of warmness/coolness of the colour, e.g. lemon yellow and cadmium yellow

When we speak of a 'colour-value' we are in fact considering the total impact of all four of these characteristics operating together. In a particular context a colour value may appear to be 'wrong' because of a failure to assess correctly one or other of these four characteristics. To continue the basic nomenclature, the 'temperature' of a colour means its apparent warmth or coolness – the man-in-the-street often refers to being 'blue' with cold or a situation being 'red-hot'.

Each colour too appears to possess a certain 'weight' both in itself and within each context. This has nothing to do with its brightness or darkness – ultramarine, for example, appears to 'weigh' more than cobalt blue, terre verte more than viridian, cadmium red slightly more than vermilion. In using colour to create expressively coherent structures this factor of weight is important.

It will be appreciated that every hue is balanced precariously between colours that are adjacent to it in terms of colour quality (e.g. red lies between a reddish-orange and a violetish-red, yellow between orange-yellow and yellow-green). To encourage the eye to discriminate subtleties within a severely restricted field, an attempt

plate 94
A tonal scale of nine steps from white to black, with the colours in the colour wheel put into their correct tonal position in relationship to the greys

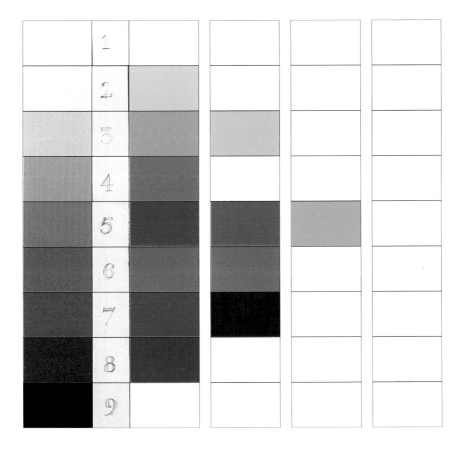

should be made to establish 'the primaries' (by mixture) – yellow, red and blue – that appear to be firmly established in the centre of their respective fields. This should be done with the greatest possible accuracy. Next establish the 'secondary' colours (i.e. those made from mixture of two primaries) – orange, green, violet – so that they too are 'central' and lean towards neither of the primaries from which they are made.

The 'tertiary' colours, the result of a mixture of a primary with a secondary, can then be mixed:

yellow	+ orange	=	yellow-orange
red	+ orange	=	red-orange
red	+ violet	=	red-violet
blue	+ violet	=	blue-violet
blue	+ green	=	blue-green
yellow	+ green	=	yellow-green

From these mixtures a 12-hue colour circle can be constructed (see plate 93). This basically is the idea which Sir Isaac Newton had of bending a spectral range of seven colours into a circle. (Seven agreed with current mystical notions of the planets and the diatonic scale in music.) Since then, physicists and chemists have constructed colour circles on red, green, blue-violet, red, yellow, sea-green, ultramarine (Ostwald); red, yellow, green, blue, purple (Munsell). However useful these may be in other respects, most practising artists are agreed upon the superiority of the trichromatic scheme for their purposes. Paul Klee writes 'The psychology of the colourist demands the division of the circle into three or six parts' and goes on to say 'division of the circle into four or eight. That really hurts!'

In discussing a simple visual unit on p. 36 it was stated that there were no absolute qualities inherent in the unit because it is continually influenced and modified by changes in its optical environment. So also in the case of colour; colour is changed by an alteration in its context, contrast being the operative factor. There is what might be called the 'energy' of colour, the dynamic factor. Gauguin wrote in a letter of 1899 – 'Think of the musical role which colour will henceforth play in modern painting. Colour which vibrates just like music, is able to attain what is most general and yet most elusive in nature – namely its inner force.'

Energy or inner force is the factor in colour of which the artist needs to be most aware. This 'energy' of colour can be well demonstrated by placing a blue square on a white field and on a black field, and then by placing a yellow square on a white field and on a black field. It will be noted that the blue on the white seems to contract and on the black it seems to expand; on the other hand, the yellow on the white seems to expand and on the black to contract.

The 'energy' is of course our own physiological reaction, since

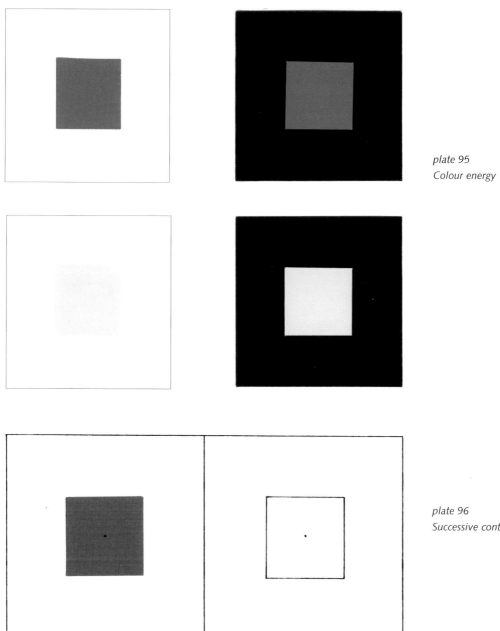

plate 95
Colour energy

plate 96
Successive contrast

even without relationship to a second colour this phenomenon operates. If we stare at a brilliant red square for some time and then close our eyes a green square appears as after-image. The unalleviated power of the red calls for the balanced relief of the complementary. This is known as 'successive contrast'.

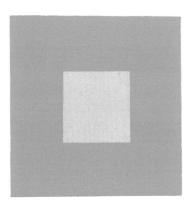

Another basic phenomenon of this kind is well demonstrated by placing a medium grey square on green and a similar square on red. In each case the grey appears to be tinged with the complementary of the colour on which it is placed. This again is an example of the same kind of physiological reaction and is known as 'simultaneous contrast'.

A distinction is often made between chromatic and achromatic colours; chromatic colours are the range of hues and their derivatives by intermixture, and achromatic colours are white, grey and black. For the painter this seems a quite useless and unnecessary complication. If one makes a collection of all the varieties of white available it will be seen that they are all tinged chromatically, some being yellowy, some bluey and the same can be said about the varieties of black. Not only is grey producible as a derivative by intermixture of all the three primaries, or pairs of complementaries plus white, but, by virtue of the simultaneous contrast phenomenon, every so-called neutral grey is likely to be chromatically influenced. Furthermore the post-impressionist use of black, white and grey place them firmly on the same footing as the chromatic colours. For the purposes of this book no distinction will be made; the word *colours* will refer to the hues and their derivatives by intermixture and to white and black. The addition of white and black means that the brightness/darkness range has been extended to its limits.

Extended work in colour mixing should be carried out both in abstract terms and in colour analysis from nature.

Two particularly valuable ways of systematically examining the possible range of colour mixtures are:

1 To take any two colours and place them opposite each other at the outer ends of a horizontal strip, and place graduated mixtures in sequence towards a middle which is occupied by a 50–50 mixture of the two. Having completed this, graduate each of these mixtures vertically, upwards towards white and downwards towards black (see plate 98).
2 To construct a network of equilateral triangles on the plan illustrated in plate 99a and develop each triangle on the basis shown in plate 99b. Out of the whole exercise will come 34 identifiably different colours.

An even more arduous colour-mixing experiment can be devised by mixing each colour on the colour circle with every other colour in turn, setting it out on a shape 12 squares x 12 squares (plate 100).

Colour analysis from natural forms (leaves, flowers, cross-sections of fruit and vegetables, etc) should be undertaken as accurately as possible, striving to get the same colour power as exists in

plate 97 (opposite)
Simultaneous contrast

WHITE

+4W

+3W

+2W

+1W

YELLOW

+1BL

+2BL

+3BL

+4BL

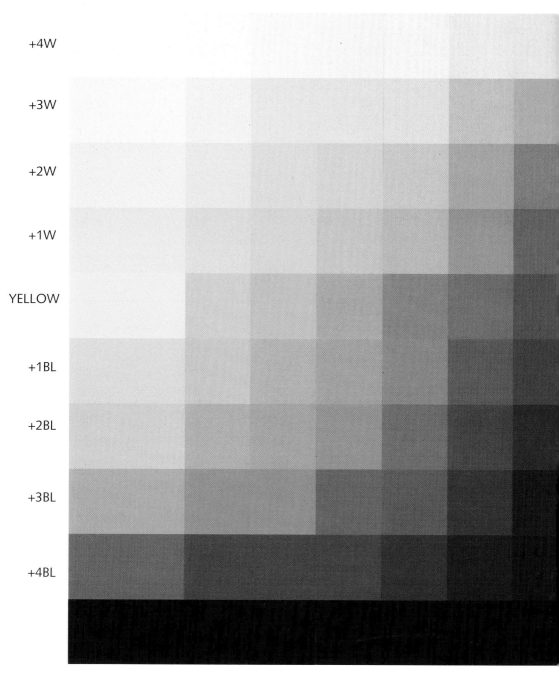

BLACK

VIOLET

plate 98
The letter symbols used are:
W = white   BL = black

The numerical figures indicate
the quantitative addition to
each mixture

plate 99a

(plate 99a is an explana-
tion of plate 99b)

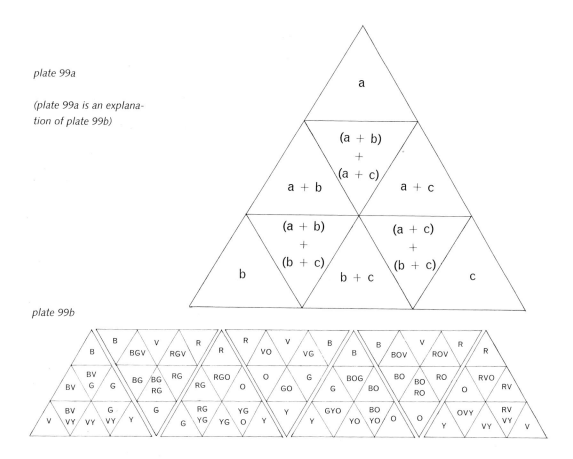

plate 99b

plates 99a, & b, 100

*In these diagrams the letter-sym-
bols are as follows:*

Y = yellow
YO = yellow-orange
O = orange
RO = red-orange
R = red
RV = red-violet
W = white
BV = blue-violet
b = blue
BG = blue-green
G = green
YG = yellow-green
V = violet
BL = black
X = 'neutral' grey

the original specimen (see plates 101a & b). This should not be done in the manner of traditional still-life painting; the aim here is not to describe the model in a certain context and under a particular condition of lighting, but to extract the colour element and study it uniquely. The model *must* be examined closely, in the hand if possible, and the colour mixtures tried out against it directly. No special attempt need be made to reproduce the botanical structure exactly since this is essentially a penetrating analysis of the colour experience. Nevertheless, some sensitive appreciation of the proportions and shape of the colour areas should be demonstrated.

It will be noticed that the term 'discord' is not used in this book. As in music, the notion of discord only occurs where fixed laws of harmony exist but, since atonality and 12-tone serialism have destroyed the old notion of discord in music, so twentieth-century developments have made the term obsolete in painting. Any colour which appears to work organically in making the constructive and expressive statements of the artist possible is valid. One may like or dislike it but there is no right or wrong in terms of absolute laws of

	Y	YO	O	RO	R	RV	V	BV	B	BG	G	YG
V	✕	V/YO	V/O	V/RO	V/R	V/RV	V/V	V/BV	V/B	V/BG	V/G	V/YG
BV	BV/Y	✕	BV/O	BV/RO	BV/R	BV/RV	BV/V	BV	BV/B	BV/BG	BV/G	BV/YG
B	B/Y	B/YO	✕	B/RO	B/R	B/RV	B/V	B/BV	B	B/BG	B/G	B/YG
BG	BG/Y	BG/YO	BG/O	✕	BG/R	BG/RV	BG/V	BG/BV	BG/B	BG	BG/G	BG/YG
G	G/Y	G/YO	G/O	G/RO	✕	G/RV	G/V	G/BV	G/B	G/BG	G	G/YG
YG	YG/Y	YG/YO	YG/O	YG/RO	YG/R	✕	YG/V	YG/BV	YG/B	YG/BG	YG/G	YG
Y	Y	Y/YO	Y/O	Y/RO	Y/R	Y/RV	✕	Y/BV	Y/B	Y/BG	Y/G	Y/YG
YO	YO/Y	YO	YO/O	YO/RO	YO/R	YO/RV	YO/V	✕	YO/B	YO/BG	YO/G	YO/YG
O	O/Y	O/YO	O	O/RO	O/R	O/RV	O/V	O/BV	✕	O/BG	O/G	O/YG
RO	RO/Y	RO/YO	RO/O	RO	RO/R	RO/RV	RO/V	RO/BV	RO/B	✕	RO/G	RO/YG
R	R/Y	R/YO	R/O	R/RO	R	R/RV	R/V	R/BV	R/B	R/BG	✕	R/YG
RV	RV/Y	RV/YO	RV/O	RV/RO	RV/R	RV	RV/V	RV/BV	RV/B	RV/BG	RV/G	✕

plate 100

harmony. The dreary banalities that proceed from theories of 'analogous' (neighbouring hues on the colour wheel), of 'triadic' (hues found at the angles of any triangle having two equal sides placed in the colour wheel) and of 'dominant' harmonies (one hue dominating the colours used, a little of it being added to everything to take the 'bite' out of every contrast) are now of interest only to fifth-rate interior decorators and pseudo-sophisticated amateurs. To the serious artist none of these theories of harmony is significant. What he has to study is the dynamic properties of colour and colour relationship, his own subjective preferences and his own assessment of the content of symbolism in colour.

plates 101a & b (opposite)
(a) A section through a cucumber
enlarged and intensively studied

Admittedly there are factors in colour mixing and the use of colour that will appear to incur special difficulties. It soon becomes apparent even to the most insensitive that the greater the multiplicity of pure colours the more they destroy each other in a sort of visual cacophony unless they are superbly organised in area, juxtaposition and shape; the huge Matisse collage *L'Escargot* at the Tate Gallery achieves just that consonance and explodes constrictive rules.

It will be found that to mix colours which contain cold and warm values in approximately equal amounts leads to a 'dead' mixture – the battle of the 'temperatures' ends in a sort of inert neutrality. But it should be realised that this 'dead' colour is expressively valuable and, in the hands of a fine colourist, can produce great beauty. Similarly to attempt a colour composition in which colours from one segment of the colour wheel are set in almost equal amount against colours from the diametrically opposite segment of the colour wheel tends to produce a state of unresolved tension which is extremely difficult to handle satisfactorily, though here again it has been achieved by the great colourists.

(b) Analysis of a flower head. No attempt is made to give a precise
description of the structure but the colour is matched with the greatest
care to ensure getting as near to the intensity of the colour of the natural
form as possible

CHAPTER 8

COLOUR
SPACE AND
SUBJECTIVE COLOUR

Colour contrast which controls the operation of colour-space, i.e. the sensation of space arising exclusively from the use of colour, can work in a variety of ways, through:

A light and dark opposition
B juxtaposition of hues
C warm-cold contrast
D complementary contrast
E simultaneous contrast
F contrast of proportion
G contrast in the shape of the colour areas
H contrast of degrees of saturation
I contrast in the 'texture' of the colour areas

These categories will now be considered separately.

A light and dark opposition
If we use the tonal scales constructed on pp. 105 and 118 we will find that every colour has its place relative to the greys on that scale, and the more contrasted two colours are in terms of their positions on this scale the more they will appear to split apart when they are placed side by side, producing a sensation of differing spatial positions. The light/dark contrast operates as strongly within one field of colour, e.g. light or dark tones of blue.

B juxtaposition of hues
If the pure saturated hues of the colour circle are correctly placed against their appropriate greys on the descending scale of grey values from white to black (see plate 103), it will be noted that they occur at varying levels. Contrast through juxtaposition of fully saturated hues is therefore inescapably linked to contrast through light and dark opposition. And it will be found that where juxtaposition of hues operates without any light/dark contrast, it is still virtually impossible for it to be disentangled from a warm-cold contrast.

plate 102
A print which utilises a balance of intentional and accidental processes in its making. Rectangular and square lino tiles were inked up in different colours and printed so that some colours overlapped others. This was followed by three different processes, each using torn pieces of paper:

(1) masking: pieces of paper were placed on an inked tile to block out mass of colour and a print taken

(2) collage: pieces of paper were pressed on to inked tiles and then stuck on to the print

(3) pieces of paper were pressed onto a black inked tile and then freely dabbed on the printed and collaged areas

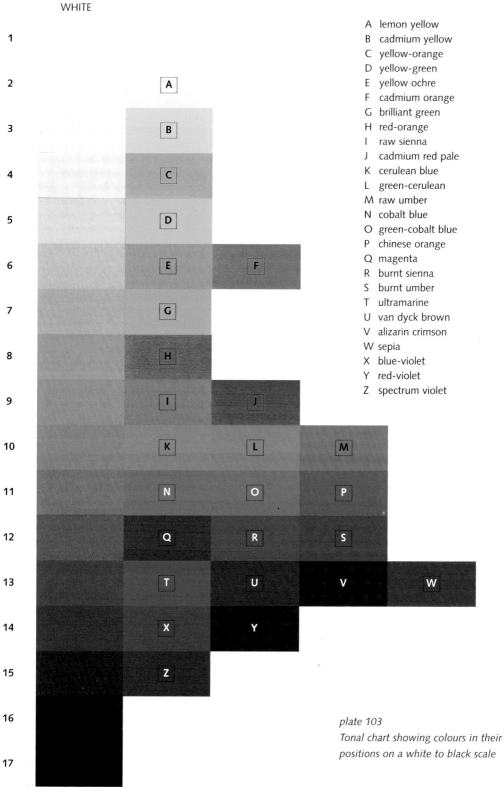

WHITE

A lemon yellow
B cadmium yellow
C yellow-orange
D yellow-green
E yellow ochre
F cadmium orange
G brilliant green
H red-orange
I raw sienna
J cadmium red pale
K cerulean blue
L green-cerulean
M raw umber
N cobalt blue
O green-cobalt blue
P chinese orange
Q magenta
R burnt sienna
S burnt umber
T ultramarine
U van dyck brown
V alizarin crimson
W sepia
X blue-violet
Y red-violet
Z spectrum violet

BLACK

plate 103
Tonal chart showing colours in their
positions on a white to black scale

C warm-cold contrast

Every colour in itself when seen alone appears to have a particular temperature value however much we may disagree about how hot or how cold we feel it to be (red-orange is clearly hot, ice-blue is at the cold extreme). In relationship with other colours we will find that its temperature is not constant (red-orange will look hotter when surrounded by cool colours than it does when surrounded by hot colours) but this is part of the superb dynamic of colour, and prevents us from making categorical statements about the operation of colour-space. It is absurd for example to say that blue is a cold colour and will always appear to recede; it depends entirely on its chroma value, brightness, the character and size of the shape it occupies, its texture as pigment and the colours that surround it in its particular context. And yet it is a useful generalisation to say that in most situations cold colours will appear recessive and contractive and hot colours emergent and expansive. The apparent spatial position of a form may often be effectively changed by altering the temperature of its colour.

plate 104a & b
Warm-cold contrast

The same red-violet looks warm at the top (because the adjacent hues are colder) and cold at the bottom (because the adjacent hues are warmer)

plate 105
Red-orange on cobalt blue and red-orange on alizarin crimson

D complementary contrast

The temperature relationship of colour naturally leads on to complementary contrast because every pair of complementaries exemplifies a balancing of cool and warm. The complementary is the colour which directly compensates any given colour, to imply in their relationship the full colour complement.

The complementary:

of red	=	yellow + blue	=	green
of yellow	=	blue + red	=	violet
of blue	=	red + yellow	=	orange

It must not be thought that complementaries exist only on the level of primary and secondary colours; for every colour there exists a complementary. There are two tests of their correctness; firstly, that mixed together the colour and its complementary should result in a 'neutral' grey-black (neutral implying no tendency towards any definite colour field); secondly, their juxtaposition gives maximum heightened vitality to each. It is one of the dynamic features of complementaries that they key each other up to maximum energy or vividness.

The establishing of these complementaries is not easy but neither is the balance of a colour and its complementary. This balance is not in the form of an equation of equal units; it will be found that blue needs a far greater area of its complementary orange, red needs an area roughly equal of green, and yellow needs a relatively very small area of violet to create a visual equilibrium (see plate 106).

The chromatic greys which can be produced by mixing comple-

1/2   1/2   1/3   2/3

plate 106
complementary contrast

1/4   3/4

Y R B

V G O

plate 107
Each of the primary colours (yellow, red and blue) are placed at the top of a chain of twelve squares. Their complementary secondaries (purple, green and orange) are placed at the opposite end of the chain. The squares are filled with progressively larger amounts of the colour towards which movement is being made. An immense range of subtle colours becomes apparent from the most restricted palette

red-orange   blue-green   yellow-orange   blue-violet

yellow-green   red-violet

plate 108
Pairs of complementary opposites

mentaries and breaking them down with white are particularly rich. Many of the subtle chromatic greys found in the work of Seurat and the Pointillists are the product of juxtaposing dots of pure complementary colours. Van Gogh's work is full of examples of the subtle use of complementaries.

E simultaneous contrast

The principle of simultaneous contrast is the painter's most important instrument of colour. He needs to develop a heightened sensitivity to the action that juxtaposed colours have upon each other. They can be made to increase mutual intensity as in the case of complementaries, they can lie so comfortably next to each other that the eye moves effortlessly across them scarcely conscious of change, they can 'shout' together, they can 'weep' together, they can 'kill' each other. Ceaseless experiment with colour juxtapositions and sequences of colour, to note the structural and expressive quality of their interactions and vibrances, is strongly recommended. The influence of the induced colour associated with the phenomenon of simultaneous contrast (see p. 108) in certain contexts can create increased excitation, in other contexts a suppression of vibrancy.

F contrast of proportion

The reference to the balancing of areas of colour brings us to the general discussion of contrast of colour area. The size of an area occupied by a colour can be a factor in its effective energy and its apparent spatial position. A principle of compensation seems to work in the fact that, with a reduction in the area covered, the

red-orange on blue-violet

red-orange on yellow-orange

plate 109
Simultaneous contrast.
Complementary opposite back-
ground colours, showing the rela-
tivity of colour by how much a
colour is dependent on its con-
text, as each centre colour
changes according to the back-
ground it is on

yellow-green on blue-green

yellow-green on red-orange

yellow-orange on red-violet

yellow-orange on yellow-green

plate 110 (below)
simultaneous contrast

colour appears to increase its energy. This in no way contradicts Gauguin's assertion that 'a metre of green is greener than a centimetre', but it does seem that the centimetre fights for its life with an increased vigour. Gauguin and Matisse come to mind as painters who have concerned themselves with creating space by organising the contrast of colour areas.

The transformations which took place in the evolution of some of Matisse's work (photographically recorded) relate to the organising of the size of the areas of colour, in each redrawing of the subject to retain a balance. He has said himself – 'There is an impelling proportion of colours that can induce me to change the shape of a figure or to transform my composition. Until I have achieved this proportion in all parts of the composition I strive toward it and keep on working.'

G contrast in the shape of the colour areas

Not only the size of colour area but also its shape is a significant factor in its spatial functioning. An eccentric 'star'-shape for example will not appear to keep the same position in space as a simple circular shape of the same area and colour. But experiments of this kind with various colours will show that the dynamics of shape cannot be separated from what might be called the integral dynamic of colour.

Again the spatial functioning of colour may be affected by overlapping, i.e. the order in which the colours appear to have been placed one on top of the other. The location of the colour relative to the picture field can also affect this – it is a strange fact, to be explained no doubt on psycho-physiological grounds, that colours and forms when located in the lower half of a picture area always appear slightly heavier and more emergent, i.e. nearer, than they do when placed in the upper half.

H contrast of degrees of saturation

Contrast of degrees of saturation (i.e. contrast between pure colour and diluted colour; diluted with white, with black, with grey, see plate 98) is yet another field of energies affecting colour-space. The dilution of the pure colour could of course be by admixture with other colours, but this would confuse the issue by bringing in other contrasts already mentioned; to appreciate the particular nature of this contrast chromatic dilution has been excluded. It will be noted that the diluted values appear to gain in vitality and the pure colours to lose some of their brilliance by the juxtaposition.

I contrast in the 'texture' of the colour areas

In every instance discussed so far the spatial functioning of a contrast may be affected by a contrast in the texture of the pigment

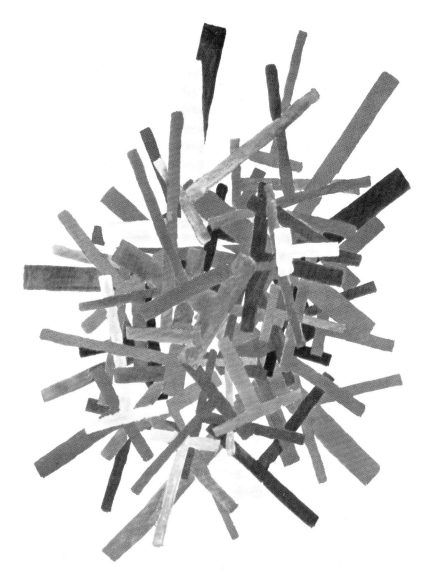

plate 111
Taking a pre-formed unit of shape (a number or a letter) work within a field of colour producing the greatest possible variety, so that the spatial energy of the colours and their relationships can be studied. In this case, red was used and extended towards red-violet on the one hand and orange on the other, care being taken to avoid trespassing into a different colour field, e.g. violet or violet-blue or orange-yellow or yellow

used. A thick impasto next to a thin liquid wash, pigment thickly textured with sand against smoothly impasted colour as in some paintings by Braque and Dubuffet; pigment spread with the palette knife against pigment applied with the brush, each will alter the apparent position of a colour in the space context.

A start has been made in the foregoing pages to assist the study of the dynamic properties of colour and colour-relationship. It needs development in as inventive a way as possible, each new manifestation being subjected to a final critical appraisal to discover and to note its particular dynamism. Plate 111 relates to much that has been discussed.

The study of one's own subjective colour preferences and the field of colour symbolism is much more elusive, admitting of little external guidance, yet it is of such fundamental importance that without it any other sort of training is almost valueless.

As a start, paint any combinations of colours at random – pure idea-less activity; from these select those that you find particularly satisfying or exciting. Also try setting down colours that express sensations of being shut in, of immobility, of laughter, of falling, of flying and so forth; or paint as you listen to music and try to get the colour to express the rhythm, the mood and the quality of what you are hearing. Colour is capable of being dramatic, lyrical, brittle, voluptuous, harsh or soothing – it can even appear to be perfumed (e.g. the superb Jackson Pollock 'Scent' 1955). The important things to *avoid* in these experiments are:

A Excessive deliberation – work at a speed natural to you and work intuitively; allow no time for the conscious mind to 'fill in' with a lot of secondhand references.
B Care in working – this is not a plea for carelessness but emphatically a plea for carefreeness. Attempts to discipline the marks made by the brush or knife will kill opportunities for experiencing effects of trailing, splash, thick and thin paint, etc.
C Attempts to 'compose' what occurs – often such difficulty is experienced in avoiding this sort of self-consciousness which introduces 'stock' recipes, that, while he was teaching, Alan Davie used to encourage his students to go to the opposite extreme and deliberately strive for the worst composition and colour effects. Out of it came unexpectedly original relationships.

From activities of this kind one enters one's own appointed field of colour creativity, one derives the confidence to move in a world of forces even more magical than the psycho-physiological 'energies' of colour perception already discussed. From it one absorbs ultimately only what is consistent with one's temperament and talent if one is a painter, what is powerfully and generally effective in terms of colour symbolism if one is a designer.

If one is concerned mainly with the organising of environment, the development of an 'environmental art' the psycho-physiological properties of lines, shapes and colours will be a large part of the substance of one's work, but for the painter it is vitally important that he does not accept this as more than the initial preparation for the pictorial or plastic statements he wants to make about his existence in the world and his reaction to it.

A painter paints to unload himself of feelings and visions
Picasso

BIBLIOGRAPHY

Additional stimulus to study and experiment will be found in the following books:

Language of Vision by Gyorgy Kepes. Doner Publications, 1995
The Thinking Eye by Paul Klee. Lund Humphries 1961
Interaction of Colours by Josef Albers. Yale University Press, 1979
The Geometry of Art & Life by Matila Costiescu Ghyka. Dover
    Publications, 1978
*The Painter's Secret Geometry by Charles Bouleau. Thames and
    Hudson, London 1963
*The Modulor by Le Corbusier. Faber, London 1954
The Art of Colour by Johannes Itten. Reinhold, New York 1974
Art and Visual Perception by Rudolf Arnheim. University of
    California Press, 1974
The Hidden Order of Art by Anton Ehrenzweig. Weidenfeld, 1993
The Bauhaus. Das Bauhaus Hans Maria Wingler. MIT, 1969
Bauhaus edited Bayer, Gropius. Museum of Modern Art,
    New York, 1976
*Printmaking-methods old and new by Gabor Peterdi. Macmillan,
    London 1960
*New Ways of Gravure by S. W. Hayter. Routledge and Kegan
    Paul, London 1949
*The New Landscape in Art and Science by Gyorgy Kepes. Paul
    Theobald and Co., Chicago 1956
On Growth and Form by D'Arcy Thompson. Cambridge University
    Press 1992
Patterns in Nature by Peter Stevens. Peregrine Books, 1974
The Divine Proportion by H E Huntley. Dover Publications, 1970
Islamic Patterns by Keith Critchlow. Thames and Hudson, 1976
The Science of Art by Martin Kemp. Yale University Press, 1990

* Available from libraries

INDEX

LIBRARY RESOURCE CENTRE
CANOLFAN ADNODDAU LLYFRGELL